ELIJAH'S WAR
PO BOX 40621
JACKSONVILLE, FLORIDA 32203-0621
Drclrileysr@gmail.com

Unless otherwise noted, a most of the Scriptures quotations are from the King James Version of the Bible.

Registered in the Library of Congress Pending
ISBN 9781657666436

Second Edition

ELIJAH'S WAR

By

DR. CARLTON LEWIS RILEY SR.

TABLE OF CONTENTS

INTRODUCTION

Why talk about the prophet Elijah and PTSD? It is a topic that is close to my heart, being a combat veteran. Initially, it was just a topic I pondered for years after I got out of the Army. One day, I encountered a retired naval soldier who said he did not have a relationship with God, and he was doomed to hell. I asked him why? He shared with me an event that took place while he was on active duty. He told me he knew he is going to hell for killing an enemy combatant while serving in Iraq.

While serving in the first Gulf War, he was a part of a Vessel Board Search & Seizure team. They were assigned to board small ships in the Gulf that looked suspicious or out of place. While on duty one day, his commander spotted a vessel that should not have been in that area near one of our Naval vessels, and his team investigated the crew. Once on-board, they went below deck to question the ship's crew as to the purpose of their travels. One of the opposing sailors pulled out a weapon forcing the naval soldier to terminate his life. His actions saved himself, along with several other naval soldiers. Once he returned stateside, his sister-in-law heard about the incident and told him by shooting an enemy combatant (to save his life along with a few other soldiers) he'd broken the sixth Commandments and was doomed to hell. I told him that was a misinterpretation of the sixth Commandment, "thou shall not kill." I shared with him the correct interpretation of the text according to the original Jewish writings. What he did is something God does not shun but expect soldiers to do to protect their families and nation. It is not God's will that anyone to perish, but it is a part of the war. In war, civilians and soldiers have to make tough decisions. I have made my peace with God concerning the choices I've made in my life, and fortunately, not to have been placed in a position that death was the only option.

More recently, I realized soldiers need to understand the bible concerning matters of war. Post-Traumatic Stress Disorder, Traumatic brain injuries, and other mentally impacting issues is a common diagnosis for soldiers returning from combat. The catalyst for publishing this book came when I was talking to a friend, asking her, "how was your weekend?" Unbeknownst to her, I had just finished my doctorate dissertation addressing the need to help soldiers challenged with combat-related PTSD, to understand God's love for soldiers. She began to share with me. One of her close friends had died over the weekend. I asked her what happen? She said her friend, who had been caring for her son, who suffered severely from PTSD. On Mother's Day 2016, her son, blatantly beat her to death with a hammer. In the subsequent weeks that followed, the media posted multiple stories of other incidents where soldiers who have PTSD randomly opened fire on civilians for no apparent reason. I witnessed a similar incidence first hand. One of the soldiers from my unit, months after our return from combat, started shooting at random soldiers from a barracks window.

The message of God's love for soldiers must be shared. We have to increase efforts to bring healing to our veterans suffering from this illness.

I never had to terminate a life, but I know people who still struggle with the physical and mental issues stemming from war. They need to know God's love for us. Sometimes, that is easier said than understood by humanity. Soldiers still question if:

- Does God truly forgive us of all sin, even murder?
- Will God judge me for following orders?
- Does God grace extend to me?

I intend to show that God Loves soldiers, even if they had to terminate a life. War brings with it a multitude of issues. There are usually no winners. The survivors sometimes wish they had died, rather than having to live with the things they've seen and experienced. God loves soldiers despite the truth that killing is a byproduct of war. If God loves and forgives us, we need to learn to love and forgive ourselves.

My objective is to express the heart of God and the love He has for soldiers who have paid the ultimate price. Their willingness to protect their loved ones by laying down their own lives or when necessary, terminating someone else's.

To address war, I must discuss the topic of death and its origin. War is hell, and I have experienced it first-hand, and I will share some of the things I've both seen and experienced. Much of what I witnessed in Panama during my combat tour, I cannot recollect. Studies show this mental blockage is a natural attempt of the mind trying to heal its self. What I do remember I share with you in this book to the best of my recollection.

As we continue, we'll look at some of the soldiers in the bible, followed by the impact war had on soldiers in biblical times. Although the diagnosis of Post-Traumatic Stress Disorder commonly called PTSD is a relatively new term compared to ancient history, it was as prevalent then as it is now. We will learn about a major prophet who suffered from this condition. The last I will take an exegesis approach to the sixth Commandment, which is just special attention to the original text, word, and meaning the writer was communicating. Lastly, we will take a look at the life of King David, who both killed and committed murder. His experience provides an excellent opportunity to see the heart of God towards killing and murder. Finally, we will close with encouraging/healing words for soldiers and their families. May God's love flow through me to reach the intended audience bringing health, healing, and understanding to a much-needed group of amazing people. Amen.

CHAPTER 1: WHO AM I - A FORMER COMBAT SOLDIER

"The love of God is far stronger than the pains of war. Amen" Dr. C.L Riley Sr.

I remember the mood after the 9/11 attacks. Most of the world watched in disbelief. Correction, we were shocked, amazed, dumbfounded, confused, and angry. After the shock wore off, we were hurt, caring, concern, worried, and looking for a way to get even. Do you know where you were (If you were born) when 9/11 took place? I was shaving getting ready for a job interview, which I was sure would be canceled due to the shocking events that were transpiring. At this point, I was a proud inactive duty civilian. During that time, General Norman Schwarzkopf provided one of my favorite quotes. After the attack, a reporter asked him if he thought there was room for forgiveness toward our attackers, he answered, "I believe that forgiving them is God's function. Our job is simply to arrange the meeting." It reminds me of words, burned into me as a combat soldier to "terminate my attackers with extreme prejudice."

As a Christian, I believe murder is wrong, but I'm called by God to protect my family and to kill only as a last result. There is a line near the end of the movie, Get Rich or Die Trying (loosely based on the life of Rapper 50 cent) where his grandmother is speaking to him. He has to perform his first major concert in a venue where there is a good possibility a rival drug dealer may try to murder him. She said, "Being a protector, that's all any man or woman is at the end of the day anyway. A protector of a child who will one day die." She expressed my views as a parent, nevertheless if at all possible, if our children must die, most parents would prefer it be by natural causes, but our greatest desires would be them living until Jesus return.

As a soldier, I felt it was my job to protect my family, who spent their lives protecting me. Before being sworn into the Army, my father died. He was aware of my plans. He wanted me to go to college. My parents didn't understand the reason I was planning to join the Army. One evening my they arranged a meeting with two members from our church to sit down and talk about my future. The meeting was with a deacon and his wife, who was a professor from Edward Waters College. They were making sure the military was the right choice for my future. I could not explain at the time my unction to join the Army. I often joked that I felt the Air Force was too much air to breathe; the Navy and Marines were too much water to drink, so the Army was perfect for me.

I knew it was the right choice for a couple of reasons. One, I felt it was a calling. Another reason was that I had so much pinned up anger in me from life's challenges. At that point in my life, I was a concern I would either implode or explode. Imploding would kill me, but exploding would kill someone else. Death by my own hands out of anger was an option I was unwilling to explore. At least in the military, I could release this anger with what James Bond called a "License to Kill." The movies don't come close to expressing the cost of taking a life nor the mental process required to follow through. Above all, when your military experience is over, we must reconcile and forgive ourselves for doing what comes naturally to some and taught to others. Soldiers must be willing to pay with our lives to preserve our love ones. Life is a gift from God given to us, but abundant life through His son is something we must choose to accept. God's love is the key to an abundant life.

I love cars, and it was not my intention to become an infantry soldier, but a military mechanic. I wanted to one day design a vehicle of my own. Going into the military was scary. Still, I was relying on the knowledge I gained from listening and observing my older brother Alan who was a former Army sniper in Vietnam and my uncle Ulysses who served in an Army Artillery unit in the Korean War. Both men I loved and respected. They did what was necessary to protect our family, and now it was time to pick up the mantle.

My initial plan was to join the Army just after high school, but my father passed away, causing me to change my plans. I joined the Army delayed entry program just to make sure my mother was okay before I left. Once I went in, I was never the same.

During basic training, while waiting at the reception station (before we went to our unit), I was boldly and blatantly disrespectful to strangers who got me started on the wrong foot. While waiting for the cattle cars (the military trucks that transported soldiers but designed initially as a transport for farm animals), another soldier and I spent an hour making fun of the old soldier sitting patiently in the sun. It was hot, and the sun beamed down on his head. Sweat rolled off his hairless scalp like he was standing in the middle of a rainstorm. We soon discovered he was one of our Drill Sergeants, and he taught us a valuable lesson. I now know what it feels like when an egg hit a hot skillet because that lesson came in the form of pushups on the blistering Georgia sidewalk for nearly an hour until the trucks arrived. It was a short ride to the barracks where I would spend the next thirteen weeks. During the trip, I reflected upon a lesson I learned from my brother. He told me the job of the Drill Sergeant is to make me into a soldier physically and psychologically. He said they would yell, use profanity, or whatever it takes to either build me up or kick me out.

When we arrived at the barracks, I heard a voice that sounds like Gunnery Sergeant Carter from Gomer Pyle U.S.M.C yelling, "Move it! Move it! Move it!" As soon as the doors of the cattle truck opened, the Drill Sergeants began beating on the side of the vehicles while yelling so loudly it made our ears ring. I said to myself, let the mind games began. Picking up our duffel bags over our heads, run up three flights of stairs; and stop next to a bunk bed. Once everyone was upstairs, we dumped out the contents of our duffel bag, and then we had to expediently place everything back into our duffel bags, run again down the three flights of stairs and get back into original formation. We ran this exercise about three times.

After the third trip, and as soon as I was back in military formation, I began to laugh because I realized this was a psychological drill. What I found so comical were the guys who were panicking and crying loudly, sobbing crocodile tears because of the pressure the Drill Sergeants were placing on us. My lead drill instructor named Drill Sergeants John Archer spotted me laughing. He snatched my sleeve as if he wanted to pull my arm completely off, forcing me to break formation. He asked if I thought this was a funny or some sort of game? I said, "yes," making a weak attempt to stop laughing. He said he ought to kick my hind parts (that's the clean version), and I said, let's do what we got to do. He sent me back to my formation and made me a squad leader. I switched places with the guy next to me and became a team leader instead.

I loved the challenges of basic training. I learned mental attitude is the basis of physical limitations. I learned this lesson from God a few months earlier before I started boot camp.

On a hot Florida day, I loaned my brother my car when I went to work. He was late picking me up. I was agitated as I walked home. Stepping out in that summer heat walking the Main Street Bridge, which spanned the St. Johns River, I felt like a buttermilk battered piece of chicken hitting a Crisco pan of hot grease. The bridge was only a third of a mile long, but I was both as warm and angry as the sun. About halfway across the bridge, I heard an internal voice that said, "if I focus on my destination and not on the heat or the weight of my combat boots, my journey was not nearly as far as it seemed." The trip was much more manageable. The journey was harder in my mind; then, it was on my body. It was all mind over matter, if I don't mind doing the task, then the obstacles to completing the job didn't matter. Lesson learned.

Eight weeks of basic training seemingly flew by (some days faster than others) but none-the-less fun. During the final days of basic training, we were called into formation to let us know our training school assignment we had chosen as our career occupation. The timing could not have been worse for my recruiter. Let me explain. I had just finished learning the basics of explosives. It was during this time that the knowledge I gained in homemade bombs was about to be applied to my recruiter. Why? When I signed up for the Army, I was under the impression that after basic training, I was going to Mechanic School. The day Drill Sergeants Archer was reading the list of people going to various schools, he called my name and said: "11X," which was any position the Army needs for an Infantry soldier. I told him he was mistaken. He verified my job code, which was 11X. He said, "11X is the job code for any infantry position the Army needed at that time, once I graduated basic."

From that moment onward, I planned to end the life of my Army recruiter. One day during a four-day weekend, I took my mom shopping at the mall, secretly looking for my recruiter. As we walked past the recruitment office, I casually glanced in to see if he was working. It was by the grace of God that my mom knew me well enough to see the mischief in my eyes. She noticed I had gotten silent as if I was thinking. She must have seen something in my eyes. At that point in my mind, I was working on the best time to make the necessary adjustments to his car that would cause him to go up in a ball of flames. My reasoning was simple. My goal was to become a career soldier, and if he was willing to screw over my life, then I was ready to put an end to his. My mom persuaded me to let him live. She said God must have had a reason, and all things will work for my good. He lived to see another day.

CHAPTER 2: A BRIEF HISTORY OF DEATH

"Everyone wants to go to heaven, but nobody wants to die." Author Unknown

Most people hate the idea that death brings an interruption to our life, work, and relationships permanently. An article I read once said it best that, "Though the inscription on many tombstones often reads "Rest in Peace," the truth of the matter is that most people do not welcome the peaceful rest of the grave. They would rather be alive and productive."

"Everyone wants to go to heaven, but no one wants to die." Death is inevitable. In the movie Meet Joe Black, although the character is a fictional view of the Grim Reaper (Death), his job seems accurate. He said, "I do not choose who dies or when they die; he is just there to collect the souls." People attempt to "cheat death," but I don't think that is possible. God extended the life of Hezekiah, but that was grace, not fate. Even as I start to write about death, it conjures up sad, negative emotions. It weighs the survivor down. In Mitch Albom book, Tuesday with Morrie, I would like to share a few ideas that I found to be true from Morrie's dying experience:

• "Death is as natural as life."

• "If we know in the end that we can ultimately have that peace with dying, then we can finally do the really hard thing, which is, make peace with living."

• "It is natural to die. We think because we're human that we're something above human…. We're not."

• "Everything that gets born dies."

One of the main issues surrounding Post Traumatic Stress Disorder is death. Either the person witnessed or feared the loss of life, death played a significant part in the trauma. So, let's take a look at death from a biblical perspective.

Death of an Animal to Cover Sin.

I loved how the late Dr. Myles Munroe taught the introduction to Genesis: In Beginning God. All other creation came after Him, "created the heavens and the earth, and the earth was without form and void, and darkness was on the face of the deep and the spirit of God was brooding over the waters and God said, 'let there be light, and there was light…" and the author goes on to describe the creative process until he gets to man.

Genesis 1:26-28, "Then God said, "Let us make mankind in our image, in our likeness, so that they may rule over the fish in the sea and the birds in the sky, over the livestock and all the wild animals, and over all the creatures that move along the ground. [27] So God created mankind in his own image, in the image of God he created them; male and female he created them. [28] God blessed them and said to them, "Be fruitful and increase in number; fill the earth and subdue it. Rule over the fish in the sea and the birds in the sky and over every living creature that moves on the ground;

Gen 2:7 "And the LORD God formed man of the dust of the ground, and breathed into his nostrils the breath of life; and man became a living being"

Gen 2:18, "And the LORD God said, "It is not good that man should be alone; I will make him a helper comparable to him."

We were created in God's image and given dominion over all creation except another man. We're not to exercise control over another person. Sin changed everything.

God told the man not to eat of the tree of the knowledge of Good and Evil. Gen 2:15- 17,

"Then the LORD God took the man and put him in the Garden of Eden to tend and keep it. [16] And the LORD God commanded the man, saying, "Of every tree of the garden you may freely eat; [17] but of the tree of the knowledge of good and evil you shall not eat, for in the day that you eat of it you shall surely die."

To be clear, what God was telling Adam was that on the day he disobeyed and ate from the tree of the knowledge of good and evil, the dying process would begin both spiritually and naturally. Eve and Adam did eat from the tree knowledge of good and evil, revealing their nakedness, which is how they became aware of sin. Sin corrupted the natural beauty of the human body as it originally appeared. The revelation came when the Glory of God departed from them. An animal had to die to cover them. Its death was the punishment humanity deserved. Bloodshed was required to cover the sin of the two creatures formed in the image of God. It is the first record of death in the bible. It was the spiritual death of man, the physical death of an animal.

Another sign that sin had entered the life of man was the Glory of God departed. What is the Glory of God? David Wilkerson says, "No man can rightly define glory, any more than he can define God. Glory is the fullness of God, and that is a subject too high for our finite minds. Yet, we do know in part." In the context of Genesis, I believe Revelations 21 explains the Glory of God best as to why Adam and Eve did not see a need to cover their bodies before sin and then the need to cover themselves afterward. Revelations 21:1-2,23-26 says:

"And I saw a new heaven and a new earth: for the first heaven and the first earth were passed away; and there was no more sea. [2] And I John saw the holy city, New Jerusalem, coming down from God out of heaven, prepared as a bride adorned for her husband; [23] And the city had no need of the sun, neither of the moon, to shine in it: for the glory of God did lighten it, and the Lamb is the light thereof. [24] And the nations of them which are saved shall walk in the light of it: and the kings of the earth do bring their glory and honour into it. [25] And the gates of it shall not be shut at all by day: for there shall be no night there. [26] And they shall bring the glory and honour of the nations into it."

God is Holy, and there is no darkness in him. He is pure light. That is why there is no night in the New Heaven and Earth because darkness does not exist in God. When He created Adam and Eve in his image, it was easy for them to reflect his glory because there was no darkness in them. Just as it says of Christ in new heaven demonstrates the glory of God.

The disappearance of the Glory of God is like the creation of a black hole in man's soul. If it seems overly complicated, please read over it and continue through the book. Here is a quick science lesson about black holes. According to NASA: "Most black holes form from the remnants of a large star that dies in a supernova explosion. A black hole is anything but space. Rather, it is a great amount of matter packed into a tiny area - think of a star ten times more massive than the Sun squeezed into a sphere approximately the diameter of New York City. The result is a gravitational field so strong that nothing, not even light, can escape." In theory, a black hole will eventually clasp on its self-leaving nothing.

Now, based on the description of a black hole, just imagine sin as synonymous with the darkness of that black hole. The prophet Isaiah describes Satan (Lucifer) in Isaiah 14:12 MSG as,

"Daystar! Son of Dawn! Flat on your face in the underworld mud, you, famous for flattening nations!

" Jesus said to his disciples in Luke 10:18, "I beheld Satan as lightning fall from heaven." Let's say that Satan is the fallen star that turned into a spiritual black hole. Once Adam and Eve entered sin, sin began to flow through their blood. The sin within humankind clasped the light of God in their being. The glory that once radiated upon them engulfed into the black hole of sin. It consumes all the natural brilliance that once shone upon them until only the darkness of sin remained.

The fall of man-caused sin to flow in our blood, leaving man caught between God's illuminating love, the black hole of sin. The illuminating love of God is far more potent than the gravitational pull of sin. The power of God is infinitely greater than sin, and his grace and glory will displace the darkness of sin before it spiritual black hole can consume His light it in and on you.

When Adam and Eve entered sin, it instantly consumed the glory of God they once reflected. They could only see the sin on their bodies. It was the first time they saw their natural bodies through the eyes of sin. Instead of seeing themselves as God viewed them, sin now tainted their thinking as Satan intended. They saw and felt the selfish, ungodly, and abnormal uses for their bodies. I believed these thoughts would have eventually driven them mad had God not intervened and put them out of the Garden of Eden where stood the tree of life.

The Glory of God, his light, is far greater than the black hole of sin within them. Psalm 92:15 says, "To shew that the Lord is upright: he is my rock, and there is no unrighteousness in him" and Psalms 5:4 says, "For thou art not a God that hath pleasure in wickedness: neither shall evil dwell with thee."

Just as sin consumes the glorious residue that once shone upon Adam and Eve, sin tries to absorb God's glory in their presence. Still, sin battles with the pure infinite light and love of His presence, pounding away at innocence until there is no trace of purity within them. Sin strives to remove all traces of godlikeness within much like a black hole clasping in upon itself.

God's goodness is his glory; and he will have us to know him by the beauty of his mercy, more than by the glory of his majesty. It is for this very reason that Moses, who God called a friend, was unable to look God directly in his face but was only able to see his hinders parts, according to Exodus 33:23. God loves us. He wants us to live an abundantly healthy life. If we stay in sin, it will consume us like a black hole leaving nothing.

Death was God's remedy to limiting what could have doomed man to an eternal war with sin. Satan declared war on God's beloved man, who is more powerful than him. Sacrificial animal skins were needed to cover sin. They were the actual first casualties of war.

God sacrificed an Animal.

God sacrificed an animal to covered Adam and Eve as their nakedness was the first corrupted unholy vision of themselves. Genesis 3:21 says, "And the Lord God clothed Adam and his wife with garments made from skins of animals." The giver of life sacrificed an animal as a temporary solution to preserve humanity until we receive a permanent cure for sin from God in the form of Jesus Christ. You are an eternal being from the very beginning of our creation, which is the reason the Tree of Life was in the Garden. Death was not a part of existence before sin, but afterward, its inclusion into the process of earth's presence is what we now call the Cycle of Life. Since the tree of life was able to regenerate their natural bodies, sin would live forever, and they would never be able to reflect the Glory of God again without a permeant remedy.

Our life force is in the blood. The shedding of the innocent blood from an animal was needed to slow men's sin consciousness until a cure would come. Sin tainted our blood, and death came into existence after man sinned.

Innocent blood covered the sin of man. Only through sacrificial shedding of innocent blood could humankind once again reflect the glory of God. That new innocent bloodline came in the form of Jesus the Christ, as we will discuss later.

Death of a Human because of jealousy

Previously we read how God killed an animal to cover the sin of man. Next, we will look at the first biblically documented death of man killing man. Once Adam and Eve were put out of the Garden of Eden, they gave birth to two sons named Cane and Able. Gen 4:1-11 says:

"Then Adam had sexual intercourse with Eve his wife, and she conceived and gave birth to a son, Cain (meaning "I have created"). For, as she said, "With God's help, I have created a man!" [2] Her next child was his brother, Abel. Abel became a shepherd, while Cain was a farmer. [3] At harvest time Cain brought the Lord a gift of his farm produce, [4] and Abel brought the fatty cuts of meat from his best lambs, and presented them to the Lord. And the Lord accepted Abel's offering, [5] but not Cain's. This made Cain both dejected and very angry, and his face grew dark with fury. [6] "Why are you angry?" the Lord asked him. "Why is your face so dark with rage? [7] It can be bright with joy if you will do what you should!

But if you refuse to obey, watch out. Sin is waiting to attack you, longing to destroy you. But you can conquer it!" [8] One day Cain suggested to his brother, "Let's go out into the fields." And while they were together there, Cain attacked and killed his brother. [9] But afterwards the Lord asked Cain, "Where is your brother? Where is Abel?" "How should I know?" Cain retorted. "Am I supposed to keep track of him wherever he goes?" [10] But the Lord said, "Your brother's blood calls to me from the ground. What have you done? [11] You are hereby banished from this ground which you have defiled with your brother's blood."

When Cain killed Abel, it first an emotional decision. For Cain, killing Able was not a life or death situation meaning they could have continued to co-exist. Able was not a physical threat to Cain. Cain's life was not in danger, nor was there a need for Cain to protect his family, but he killed his brother simply because he was angry and wanted the praise that his brother received from God. God calls this was murder. No man had ever died, and Author Gene Getz said Cain did not know his brother would die. Nevertheless, God punished him to correct his behavior because Cain made a decision that affected his brother's blood (releasing it from his body), which ultimately made Abel the first man to die.

By destroying the blood that flows through a creature and stops it from either completing the circulatory system in the body or alter the composition of the blood (removing the oxygen; remove cells that fight off contaminants in the blood, etc.) will cause the human body to stop living. By cutting off the oxygen carried throughout the blood, you cut off life itself. Cain and Abel co-existed without issues until Cain allowed jealousy to push him into a rage causing Abel's blood to stop flowing within his body and pour out on the ground. The first death of a man.

Death of humankind by a flood: The Wickedness

Just as God intervenes to prevent Adam and Eve from terminating a life before they were able to populate the earth, God once again had to act on man's behalf. Although He delayed man's self-destructive nature, ungodly interactions between the sons of God (angels) and women complicated God's plans for the man He created. It is at this point that God numbered man's days. It appeared the children produce by Angels and women bore a significant advantage over the man God created in his image. Due to this ungodly union, the scripture says the wickedness of man grew great. According to Genesis 6:1-7:

"Now it came to pass, when men began to multiply on the face of the earth, and daughters were born to them, [2] that the sons of God saw the daughters of men, that they were beautiful; and they took wives for themselves of all whom they chose. [3] And the Lord said, "My Spirit shall not strive with man forever, for he is indeed flesh; yet his days shall be one hundred and twenty years." [4] There were giants on the earth in those days, and also afterward, when the sons of God came in to the daughters of men and they bore children to them. Those were the mighty men who were of old, men of renown. [5] Then the Lord saw that the wickedness of man was great in the earth, and that every intent of the thoughts of his heart was only evil continually. [6] And the Lord was sorry that He had made man on the earth, and He was grieved in His heart. [7] So the Lord said, "I will destroy man whom I have created from the face of the earth, both man and beast, creeping thing and birds of the air, for I am sorry that I have."

God had judged the inhabitance of land because sin had grown so rampant. Genesis 7 NKJV says,

"Then the Lord said to Noah, "Come into the ark, you and all your household, because I have seen that you are righteous before Me in this generation. [2] You shall take with you seven each of every clean animal, a male and his female; two each of animals that are unclean, a male and his female; [3] also seven each of birds of the air, male and female, to keep the species alive on the face of all the earth. [4] For after seven more days I will cause it to rain on the earth forty days and forty nights, and I will destroy from the face of the earth all living things that I have made." [5] And Noah did according to all that the Lord commanded him. [6] Noah was six hundred years old when the floodwaters were on the earth. [7] So Noah, with his sons, his wife, and his sons' wives, went into the ark because of the waters of the flood. [8] Of clean animals, of animals that are unclean, of birds, and of everything that creeps on the earth, [9] two by two they went into the ark to Noah, male and female, as God had commanded Noah. [10] And it came to pass after seven days that the waters of the flood were on the earth. [11] In the six hundredth year of Noah's life, in the second month, the seventeenth day of the month, on that day all the fountains of the great deep were broken up, and the windows of heaven were opened. [12] And the rain was on the earth forty days and forty nights. [13] On the very same day Noah and Noah's sons, Shem, Ham, and Japheth, and Noah's wife and the three wives of his sons with them, entered the ark— [14] they and every beast after its kind, all cattle after their kind, every creeping thing that creeps on the earth after its kind, and every bird after its kind, every bird of every sort. [15] And they went into the ark to Noah, two by two, of all flesh in which is the breath of life. [16] So those that entered, male and female of all flesh, went in as God had commanded him; and the Lord shut him in."

Here we find that as the floodwaters cover humanity, man lost the ability to intake the air necessary to substance life, which in turn terminated the life of everyone not protected in the ark or simply put they drowned.

Death of Soldiers who serve their country: War of the Kings

Let's look at the end of a man while trying to protect his family. A group of bandits kidnapped Abraham's family and stole his goods. He just happens to be wealthy, had a lot of servants and friends, which he asked for help. He manages to form a small army to help him regain what he lost. On the other end of the scope, we see he is fighting soldiers who are loyal to their kings. These soldiers went to war at the request of their kings. They went for the same reason that most modern-day soldiers go to war today, which is to protect your families, ideals, and beliefs. The War of Kings is the first time the term war applied in scripture, according to biblical scholars. Here is the first time in the bible we have war mentioned and commonly referred to by most biblical scholars as to the War of the Kings. Genesis 14 Amplified Bible says:

"14 In the days of the [Eastern] kings Amraphel of Shinar, Arioch of Ellasar, Chedorlaomer of Elam, and Tidal of Goiim, [2] they [invaded the Jordan Valley near the Dead Sea, and] made war with Bera king of Sodom, Birsha king of Gomorrah, Shinab king of Admah, Shemeber king of Zeboiim, and the king of Bela (that is, Zoar). [3] All of these [kings] joined together [as allies] in the Valley of Siddim (that is, the Sea of Salt). [4] Twelve years they had served Chedorlaomer [the most powerful king in the invading confederacy], but in the thirteenth year they rebelled."

As this story progresses, we see that father of Faith Abraham (Abram at this time in his life) putting together a militia to recover his nephew, snatched for his property like the movie Taken starring Liam Neems. Unannounced to the kidnapping army, Abram had "a particular set of skills," which he poured into the servants of his house and a few nearby allies. Genesis 14 says:

"[10] Now the Valley of Siddim was full of asphalt pits; and the kings of Sodom and Gomorrah fled; some fell there, and the remainder fled to the mountains. [11] Then they took all the goods of Sodom and Gomorrah, and all their provisions, and went their way. [12] They also took Lot, Abram's brother's son who dwelt in Sodom, and his goods, and departed. [13] Then one who had escaped came and told Abram the Hebrew, for he dwelt by the terebinth trees of Mamre the Amorite, brother of Eshcol and brother of Aner; and they were allies with Abram. [14] Now when Abram heard that his brother was taken captive, he armed his three hundred and eighteen trained servants who were born in his own house, and went in pursuit as far as Dan. [15] He divided his forces against them by night, and he and his servants attacked them and pursued them as far as Hobah, which is north of Damascus. [16] So he brought back all goods, and also brought back his brother Lot and his goods, as well as the women and the people.

Death of Humans by natural causes.

Death was a product of sin. It was a means to escape this corrupt fleshly body and gaining an incorruptible one if you have accepted Jesus as your Lord and Savior. As we read in Genesis chapter 5, we saw that man lived hundreds of years without the tree of life that was in the Garden of Eden before succumbing to death. God numbered man's days before the flood, and afterward, they began to die earlier than previously recorded. Humankind went from living 900 plus years to 100 plus years. Below is a list of people the bible took the liberty of sharing their ages at death. Most of them usually died from natural causes and but more importantly, not at the hands of another person.

• Sarah lived one hundred and twenty-seven years; these were the years of the life of Sarah. Genesis 23:1

• This is the sum of the years of Abraham's life which he lived: one hundred and seventy-five years. Genesis 25:7

• Jacob lived seventeen years after his arrival so that he was 147 years old at the time of his death. Genesis 47:28

• Joseph dwelt in Egypt, he and his father's household. And Joseph lived one hundred and ten years. Genesis 50:22

I need to add one final note about this chapter concerning death. During this time in history, humanity had not received the Law to God, so every man did what was right in their own eyes. Humankind could live much better lives, but poor choices lead to be shorter life spans. There was no law in the land; this leads to a very corrupt environment. According to Genesis 6:5, "Then the Lord saw that the wickedness of man was great in the earth, and that every intent of the thoughts of his heart was only evil continually." Mankind could make better decisions but did not. Noah is evidence that man could make better choices for living. Man's bad choices are what led to God, giving man the Ten Commandments to shine his light within the soul of humanity, showing us the darken condition of our hearts and providing laws to help us live better productive lives.

My first personal encounter with Death

When I was in the fifth grade, I had the privilege of being an elementary school crossing guard. It was a position of high honor because it required each student to maintain an "A" average and carry ourselves in a respectable manner that would inspire others to emulate. Best of all, the position came with a bright orange crossing guard vest with a shining badge. I was five-foot-tall with a husky frame which made me a little taller than Arnold Jackson from the television show Diff'rent Strokes complete with the chubby cheeks looking a squirrel with a mouth full of marshmallow and a nice mini-afro to match. One of the perks of being a school crossing guard was a chance to attend the pool party at the Principal houses, which he threw at the end of every school year, and I heard it was awesome. I was nearly the ideal student with my eye on the end goal in mind, the perfect party. I was experiencing an abundant life for a day.

The day of the party, the weather gearing up to be a bright, hot, rainless, and sunny day. At that point in my life, I had been to the beach but never gone swimming in a public pool, let alone a private pool. The truth is, I had never known anyone who could afford a pool in their yard, puddles yes, pools no. The Principal picked us up at the elementary school. Once we arrived at his house, everyone immediately rushed to his son's room to change into our swim trunks and off went into the vast sprinkling swimming pool in his backyard. The sunlight appeared to be dancing off each wave as they peaked from one side of the pool to the other. Once inside of the swimming pool, I climbed on top of the rubber float. I loved the water. I did not know how to swim. Life for me was terrific as I drifted across the pool, thinking, "this is how rich people lived." It was a significant departure for the sand-filled yard in the heart of the ghetto where I lived.

One of the kids from the school wanted to get on the float. I told him I could not swim, but once I get closer to the side, I would give up the raft. The second time he asked for the float, I again told him I could not swim. He started pretending he was going to flip it over. Realizing his impatience, I began to paddle my way toward the side of the pool. Without any warning, he went underneath the raft, and the next thing I knew, I was sinking beneath the beautiful waves, which were quickly becoming a watery casket. It took a moment for me to grasp what was happening. I sank beneath the waves to the bottom of the pool. It was like being the last man on the Titanic with no air or hope. The rim of the pool quickly faded from sight as I turned my focus inwardly, having a genuinely spiritual conversation with myself. I remember asking myself, "if anyone was going to save you?" Staring upwardly and judging by the lack of activity given my water-filled eyes, the answers were "no!" I could feel my heart starting to race as it seems it was my time to exit this life in hopes of a better one. After what felt like a lifetime, seeing as it appeared that no one was jumping in the pool to rescue me, I concluded within myself that this was the end. Sadly, I was not afraid of dying. I found there was no need to continue my holding my breath as if I had hope nor trying to savor the last bite of oxygen I was clinging too. With that thought in mind, I exhaled. I watched as the final air bubbles escaped from my lips like air from a rubber balloon and faced death for the first time.

I'm not sure if it was a lack of oxygen or adrenaline rushing in my brain, possibly causing me to hallucinate, but I saw my life flash before me as the life within begin to fade. Everything faded to black. The next image I saw was a person kneeling beside me; my body stretched out on the pool deck, coughing up water and gasping for air. After lying still for a few minutes, they helped me sit up. I was very disoriented and unsure of what had taken place. For the remainder of the day, I sat near the pool, churning home-made Ice cream. It was years before I went into any water above the waist level. I don't think my classmates realized he near sent me to the point of no return by flipping the raft. By separating me from the oxygen I so desperately depended on to live, I learned that death would meet you at any time in anyplace.

CHAPTER 3: SOLDIERS IN THE BIBLE

In the previous chapter, we had a brief introduction to death in the book of Genesis. We saw when Abraham went to war to recover his nephew. He gathers a militia to fight an army. In Genesis, God had people who were not yet a nation but never-the-less his children. As we consider the book of Exodus in the Old Testament and the remainder of the Bible, we see that Israel became a nation of Gods' people. After being placed in bondage in Egypt, God raised a leader named Moses to deliver them from Pharaoh's hands. When Pharaohs released God's people, then began to pursue them into the wilderness with his army, God became Israel's defender. Israel is God's people. They're (later the gentiles were included) his family and friends, which he vowed to protect. He was the Commander and Chief of Israel, and he set the example for every other soldier of Israel to follow. What did God do?

When he delivered the children of Israel, it was He who drown Pharaoh's army in the Red Sea. Exodus 15:1-7 AMP says

"[1]Then Moses and the children of Israel sang this song to the Lord, singing,

"I will sing to the Lord, for He has triumphed gloriously; The horse and its rider He has thrown into the sea.[2] "The Lord is my strength and my song, And He has become my salvation;
This is my God, and I will praise Him; My father's God, and I will exalt Him. [3] "The Lord is a warrior; The Lord is His name.[4] "Pharaoh's chariots and his army He has thrown into the sea;
His chosen captains are drowned in the Red Sea. [5] "The deep [water] covers them; [Clad in armor] they sank into the depths like a stone. [6] "Your right hand, O Lord, is glorious in power;
Your right hand, O Lord, shatters the enemy. [7] "In the greatness of Your majesty You overthrow and annihilate those [adversaries] who rise [in rebellion] against You; You send out Your fury, and it consumes them like chaff."

Once God delivered his people from Pharaoh, He charged them to protect their freedom, lives, families, and possession just as had done to free them. The Bible goes to provide other soldiers who risked their lives, and many died living up to the example God set in protecting the nation of Israel.

In the movie, American Sniper, there is some dialog between Wayne Kyle (father of the American Sniper) and Chris Kyle his son showing the need for soldiers and law enforcement:

Wayne Kyle: [to his sons] There are three types of people in this world: sheep, wolves, and sheepdogs. Some people prefer to believe that evil doesn't exist in the world, and if it ever darkened their doorstep, they wouldn't know how to protect themselves. Those are the sheep.

Wayne Kyle: Then you've got predators who use violence to prey on the weak. They're the wolves.

Wayne Kyle: And then there are those blessed with the gift of aggression, an overpowering need to protect the flock. These men are the rare breed who live to confront the wolf. They are the sheepdog.

I've taken the liberty of introducing a few of these leaders or "sheepdogs" to you from the Bible. God also raised judges to protect Israel. God made sure we were aware that soldiers could be male or female, left-handed or right, part of the nation by birth or marriage. Regardless of who they were or where they were from, they protected Israel.

• Samson is one of the most renowned soldiers in the Bible. Raised a Nazarite, but he had a fatal fondness for Philistine women. Samson was a man of immense strength who killed a lion with his bare hands. He also eliminated a thousand Philistines with a jawbone of an ass. Samson was brought down by a Philistine girl named Delilah. She discovered that his uncut hair was the source of his strength. She had him blinded and imprisoned at Gaza. Samson repented, called out to God, who returned his might. Positioned between two primary stone columns, he pulled down the Temple of Dagon, killing himself while taking the life of his enemies. That day Samson killed about 3,000 Philistines.

• Ehud was a left-handed Benjaminite who personally killed Eglon king of Moab and ended Moabite domination of Israel.

• Othniel was the first warrior/Judge of Israel. He delivered Israel from the oppression of the Edomites.

• Shamgar was an ordinary farmer turned citizen-soldier who was tired of the enemy soldiers plundering his land to put an end to it he killed 600 Philistines with an ox goad.

• Deborah was a prophetess and a judge. She and General Barak defeated Sisera, the general of the army of Canaanite King Jabin of Hazor at the Battle of Kishon near Mt Tabor.

• Jael was a soldier during the battle, which was led by Deborah and Barak. He was the soldier who credited with winning the fight. While General Sisera was taking a nap, Jael drove a tent peg through his head. End of war.

• Gideon was a fearful, reluctant soldier whom the Angel of the

Lord appeared to at Ophrah. He sought confirmation of God's will twice for a sign by putting out a fleece. Feeling confident that God was with him, Gideon, on God's command, reduced the size of his army from 32,000 to 300 and successfully defeated the Midianite army.

• If we can see God as the Commander and Chief, then Moses was Chairman of the Joint Chief of Staff. Moses is called one of the greatest men of the Old Testament. Being raised as an Egyptian Prince and he was well-groomed, exceptionally well trained in Military leadership. As a leader for God, he starts off his career by taking down an Egyptian, then becomes God's emissary as the Israelites delivered from slavery. Moses served as a military leader through many of the attacks from neighboring tribes as they wandered through the wilderness.

• Joab was a general in David's army.

• Joshua becomes the earthly Commander-and-Chief after Moses died. He leads the Israelites in a bloody campaign to take possession of the Promised Land, but he is best known for leading Israel to victory against Jericho.

• King David is best known for his duel against the giant Goliath. He was a poet, musician, and a skilled warrior — one gets the impression that King Saul wasn't the only one with murderous jealousy of the guy.

These are just a few of the soldiers in the Old Testament. In the New Testament, Jesus commanded a Centurion for his faith, found in Matthew 8:5-13. If all soldiers were hell-bound degenerates, then God would not have included them in the Bible, let alone mention them in both the Old and New Testaments. Many received mention in the Heroes of faith in Hebrew. Rick Warren, the author of the Purpose Driven Life, said that "So I would say God hates war, but God loves every soldier." I will provide more information on God's view of veterans in later chapters.

Next, we will look at my transitions from army training to a combat soldier.

CHAPTER 4: LOCK AND LOADED- OPERATION JUST CAUSE

In 1983 General Manuel Noriega seized control of his country once he became head of the National Guard in Panama. After he obtained a position of power, he grew the military while manipulating the election so that he could control the winning president like his puppet leader. Under his reign, corruption was widespread, and he used his power to imprison and sometimes kill anyone who opposed him. In 1987 one of Noriega's former officers publicly accused of cooperating with Colombian drug producers. Responding to the accusation, the US imposed strict sanctions, which eventually took an exacting toll on his country. President George Bush ordered Operation Just Cause, an invasion consisting of over 25,000 soldiers following the shooting of a U.S. Marine.

I was a member of the 7th Infantry Division in Fort Ord California at that time. My unit was the Forth Battalion Seventh Infantry, known as the Buffalo Soldiers. During my time there, I faced quite a few life or death situations, but one stands out. Landing in the country was not unlike what I'd seen in the movies as soldiers arriving in Vietnam Nam. We landed in a tropical paradise complete with an oceanside base, palm trees, and plenty of sunshine. When I arrived in Panama, I had one primary objective, which was to come home alive. I was not passing that responsibility to anyone else. A few days later, we headed out to a training base to prepare for Jungle warfare. Climbing onto a half-ton truck, they asked for volunteers to be the gunner? The gunner was the person standing up behind the M60 machine gun mounted on top of the cab of the troop transport truck. I would be the first line of defense if the convoy were to come under attack. We arrived at the training base safely as news media continued to talk about our presence in Panama.

It seemed surreal sitting on the shores of Fort Sherman looking across the water at the beautifully lite city of Colón Panama. I remember sitting on the coastline talking with a friend unsure of what God had in store for our futures, but we were sure that there was no turning back, and death would not take us without a fight. It's hard to express the contrast between our locations and our thoughts. Listening to the soothing sounds of waves gently rolling up the shore, stopping and gliding back out, leaving the sound of dissipating seam foam misting away against tumultuous internal thoughts. We reflected on the choices we made and events in our lives leading up to the unnerving, unknown, and possible outcome of this war while our hearts raced with uncertainty. From that moment onward, we left life before Panama behind and focused on our lives as a soldier, with one objective, make it home alive with our military brothers with whom we'd arrived in the country.

The night the first shoot was fired plays clearly in my mind. There was nothing special about the day. Eat, train, and wait for war. In the states, this was routine, except war was not looming. Now the sun has set, no American televisions or radios of entertainment value. Cell phones were few and far between for only people who could afford them. One by one, my barrack brothers were filtering bags into our rooms. There were twelve of us hanging out together in the barracks for the first time since we arrived in the country. We were laughing, talking, and reminiscing about military experiences.

The conversations shifted to music. About mid-verse into a seventy-rock song, my First Sergeant walked past the door of our room and said, "It's On!" That's it. No other words or explanations stated, but none was needed. Unequivocally we understood, "It's time to fulfill our commitment to our country. Be it life or death; we're going to war!" After he spoke, the room went silent. No one said another word. We put on our battle dress jackets, gatherer our necessities, and swiftly moved through the hall to the operation center as if death was on our trails, and we were not going to let him catch us. It all seemed dreamlike as we walked into the ammo room and started loading our M16 clips. No one uttered a peep. The room filled with stone face soldiers speed loading our weapons. The room filled with stone face soldiers speed loading our weapons. The smell of brass and gun oil filled the room as the click, click, clicking sound of infantry force-feeding rounds into our 30 round magazines. There was a symphony of sound. The room smelled of brass filled the air as we fed rounds into the M-16 magazine, empty ammo pouch replaced by full ones and metal clips which guided the bullets into the clip hitting the table and floor filled our ears.

My next stop was the radio room where I had been working since we arrived. I was the S2/Intelligence Clerk back in garrison, but when we were out in the field, I was the Security Officer Radio Operator. Once I had all my combat gear on and ready, I stepped into the TOC, which stood for Tactical Operation Center. Then came the hardest part, we played the waiting game, but we did not have to wait very long. I was standing a few feet away from the radio when the call came in that the Panamanian Defensive Force was starting to stir, and my Coronel gave the order to fire at will. It was "ON!"

The sound of gunfire rang out over the radio as I waited for the battle to reach our location. My assignment was a security position out of the Command room. Adrenaline rushed through my veins, and I felt focused and alive. There were two of us, and we quickly established our field of fire. It was all second nature. No need to think it was all instinctive.

Within moments the earth rumbled beneath us as we felt the bombshell going off in the distance. It seemed as if the world was coming to an end as I watched the cities going up in flames. We were only two hours into the battle when I received word of the first casualty of war from my unit. His name was Specialist Gibbs. I had spoken to him earlier that day about Christ, which is something I rarely did. I struggle with letting go of my whole life to Christ back then. At that moment, I felt an unction to ask him about Christ. He told me his relationship was good. It was good to reflect upon our last conversation, it didn't stop the hurting, but I quickly shift my focus back to stay alive. His death to me was a very vibrant reminder that this war was real, and Death is on his job, so I better stay on mine.

It's hard to rest when there is no peace in sight.

I survived the initial battle, but as long as I stood on the foreign ground, it was not over for me. We remained on high alert. Only exhaustion could put a soldier to sleep during the war. I trust the guy's in my unit. Our bonds as soldiers go far beyond any relationship I have ever experienced. The only thing that comes close either before or after other is my relationship with Christ. A few days after the first battle, we moved from the TOC toward downtown Colón Panama.

I must admit that I had watched a lot of war movies growing up, but nothing could prepare me for being in an active war zone. As we moved from location to location, we made various stops looking for any remaining opposition soldiers. With all the walking we'd done, we should have been tired, but we weren't. Fatigued was blocked by adrenalin. We stopped at an abandoned school. Our first job was to clear the building. Securing the building involved intensively checking the property with our weapons ready to terminate any Panamanian Defense force personnel, guaranteeing we were alone for a momentary rest. I can honestly say from experience; it's hard to rest when there is no peace in sight. I tried to image the school once filled with the hopes and dreams of young people excited about the impact they will have upon the world, but the disheveled grounds and eerie silence quickly forced me back to reality.

Using only hand signals, we cleared each classroom. I saw rooms filled with tables and desks jostled about — chairs scattered in abstract piles. Artwork hung on the walls. Daily and weekly assignments still covered the chalkboards, but it looked as if a riot had broken out, and school ended abruptly. It was a dismal sight. I was standing in a place once filled with aspiring future leaders whose dreams of greatness had deserted the school grounds, each classroom empty, leaving only hopelessness. Once we cleared the building, a few of my brothers we posted in various locations around the school grounds as Sentries. We waited on orders for our next move. We received orders to continue towards Colón.

The smell of death and war was in the air everywhere as we drew closer to the city. There was nearly no movement as far as the eye could see. Nearby, there were smoldering fires all around. I saw buildings covered in the faded color scheme of the previous decades. Shattered glass covered the sidewalks, buildings perforated with bullet holes and concrete columns, with huge chunks missing revealing the rebar within. All that remained was desolate streets and alleys. Cars smashed, crushed, and riddled with holes covered the roads. I saw the back end of cars and trucks perturbing out of buildings as if it had been a Hollywood stunt, only the dead bodies were still inside, and they were not actors. As we entered the city, there was a minimal movement amongst civilians, and God forbid if we saw a soldier other than American.

We traveled with our weapons prepared to fire at anything that moved in a manner to harm us. Every street was litter with trash and smoke. Eventually, army trucks arrived as we drove directly into the city, not stopping for anything.

We ultimately arrived at our new headquarters. Another team had come and swept the building rendering it safe to set up shop. We were still hearing gunfire going off in the distance as we were setting up. Our headquarters was in the city of Colón, Panama, formerly City hall. The initial adrenaline rush started to slow down. It took a few days before we began to see Panamanian citizens coming out of their homes and hiding place, on to the street during the daylight hours as the city was under curfew. It was evident that the people were glad Noriega's tyrannous government was ousted. I was amazed at the resilience of the people as they slowly began to mill around their war-torn a few days after the attack began.

Amid war, I also saw things that were beautiful or just outright astonishing. I have seen sights you would have had been there to believe. Have you ever seen a car being carried down the street on the front of a forklift? I have. On Christmas Day, we received care packages from the States. Although it appeared to be, it was not safe to be in public downtown Panama, but I experienced one of the purest joyful memories in my life. As a soldier filed in and out of my briefing area, I asked if they mind if we gave their care-packages filled with candy to the local kids? Most were glad to give their candy away. A friend and I threw candy out of the second-floor windows to every kid we saw. They came from all over the city. I knew there was a lot of looting going on because all the kids were wearing new sneakers. That euphoric feeling did not last long.

About a week after we had been City hall, I had a real life-changing experience. A Captain sent me on what I could only call a secret mission. I received orders to escort two Army Officers' wives and their kids (stationed in Panama) to the nearest military base commissary to get food and supplies because they had run out. The Captain assigned me the task of being their escort. Still, he failed to communicate to our local security checkpoint that I would be leaving the city in a private car and returning later. I don't remember how long the trip last. I was full of adrenaline getting in this private car, going on missions with no means of communication with anyone, to a destination that I did not know or how to get there. I followed the orders given to me. Thank God for Jesus. The drive out of downtown Colón where my unit had set up headquarters in the old city hall, was quiet and uneventful until we reached the gate to the base of the commissary. As we approached the base entrance, I notice the MP's with their handguns and m16's drawn facing the wood line to my left.

The primary battle was over. However, Noriega was still on

the run, and we were still dealing with small skirmishes from Panamanian Defense Forces who were still shooting at American soldiers. Once again, since we first entered the city, it seemed surreal driving on a deserted highway no other visible vehicles in either direction for miles. On the drive from Colón to closed military commissary, I knew the number of lives lost during the conflict was wrong, as reported by media. Their assessment was consistently low. I saw three small mountains of dead bodies, seemingly two stories high each waiting to be buried bodies in mass graves. According to one news report, "Disagreement exists over how many civilians perished. Washington claimed that few died. In the "low hundreds," the Pentagon's Southern Command said. But others charged that US officials didn't bother to count the dead in El Chorrillo, a poor Panama City barrio that US planes possibly indiscriminately bombed based on intelligence reports that it was considered a bastion of support for Noriega. According to Grassroots, human-rights organizations reported thousands of civilians killed and tens of thousands displaced. I found this to be credible information. The conflicting report troubled me for years. The first time I watched a documentary about the after-effects of "Operation Just Cause" ten years after it was over, I cried. It troubled me for years, but by God's grace, I overcame the shame, horrors, and atrocities that had taken place during my short tour.

The military police waved us onto the base. When we reached the commissary, the ladies went inside to get what they needed while I stood guard over the car. Once the wives returned to the car, I was asked by one of the women if we could take food to a family member? Divert our mission to drop off necessities to some of their family members whom they said would die without it was not an option. I chose to stick to the original mission. It was the right choice.

As we left the commissary, it appeared the MP's had gotten their targets as we drove off the base because they were no longer skewering the forest that surrounded the base checkpoint with their weapons intensely pointed and eyes focused looking for movement. As we were returning to Colón city from the commissary, I learned beliefs could be a matter of life and death. We approached the bottleneck. This area called the bottleneck due to Colón Panama being a peninsula. As you drive into the city, the road narrows like the neck of a soda bottle, making it the perfect place for a military security checkpoint. As we drove towards the inspection point, I realize something was seriously wrong. There were more than the usual number of soldiers at the entry point. The situation was undoubtedly getting worse because a Hummer filled with more soldiers pulled into the checkpoint, soldiers jumped out and started aiming their weapons in our directions. A firefight would soon ensue.

At first, I thought an enemy vehicle was behind us, but a glance into the rear-view mirror and looking over my shoulder, I realized that assumption was wrong. I quickly concluded that our vehicle was deemed unfriendly. I realized they were not just aiming in our direction, the soldiers were pointing their weapons at our car, and it all seemed unreal. I checked behind us again, hoping for a cause for the soldiers' actions. When I looked out of the back window and saw that no one was following us, not even from a distance, I told the driver to stop the car.

Why they focused on my car, I'm not sure. Maybe it was the muzzle of my M16 extended from the car window that caught their attention. Perhaps it was a lack of communication from the Captain who sent me out of the city without proper notification placed me in this life-threatening predicament.

My first thought that morning was not "today is a good day to die" although death never seems far away at war. My goal was to trust God that I stayed one step ahead of Death himself. I knew we would be returning into that back through the bottleneck. We (the guys in my unit) were all fill intense anxiety. I was unmistakably in a war. It was not a movie set, filled with directors, cameras, stuntmen, and movie trailers. We were real soldiers, fighting a real enemy, with real bullets, real civilians surrounded by real death. None of us were planning to die, although I began to relive the feelings I experienced when I nearly drowned at age ten.

I immediately told the driver to stop the car with clear short, deliberate words. Seeing my eyes fixed forward, the driver realized at that moment what I already knew. The soldiers were planning to kill us. The women started screaming and crying out loud, "Nos Vamos a morir," meaning "We're going to die!" in Spanish. I repeatedly told them we're going to be okay, but inside I was thinking, "God, I hope they're ready to meet you." These were not just any soldiers we were facing. They were my teammates. We were fighting for our survival at a few days before this situation, striving to protect each other so we could get back to our loved ones. They were my military brothers from other mothers. It was at that moment that I called out to God in a silent prayer asking for direction. It was not the first time I faced death.

In the fifth grade, I did not have the wisdom to cry out to God, but by this point in my life, I knew where my help came. An internal voice (I believe it was God) instructed me to take off my Kevlar helmet, put it over the muzzle of my weapon, which was sticking out of the window. Next, I slowly open the front passenger side door where I was sitting. With my arms extended, my m16 parallel to my body with a helmet covering the muzzle, I slowly walked the car through the checkpoint. Once they guys recognized me as friendly, they began to stand down. Some of them tried to speak to me, but I was so angry I could not say a word. I just kept walking. I went to the old city hall my unit had commandeered and had a close look at life. We had safely made it back to the command center by the grace and directions of a loving God.

I was in Panama a little over ninety days and can't begin to express my sorrow for soldiers doing multiple tours in the Middle East. Operation Just Cause was one of the most successful military actions in US history from a tactical point of view. In terms of what I experienced, one investigative team said, "The University of Panama's seismograph marked 442 major explosions in the first 12 hours of the invasion, about one major bomb blast every two minutes. Fires engulfed the mostly wooden homes, destroying about 4,000 residences. Some residents began to call El Chorrillo "Guernica" or "little Hiroshima." Shortly after hostilities ended, bulldozers excavated mass graves and shoveled in the bodies. "Buried like dogs," said the mother of one of the civilian dead."

The mission was controversial due to the resulting in some government counts the loss of hundreds (thousands) of Panamanian lives and the subsequent damage to Panama City and El Chorillo. The military was able to achieve its goals quickly. Noriega surrendered, was taken to the US, tried, convicted, and jailed on drug trafficking charges. News media sources said Noriega died May 29, 2017, of complications from brain surgery. Twenty-seven years ago, on the morning of December 20, 1989, President George H.W.

Bush launched Operation Just Cause. We were sent on a mission to execute a warrant of arrest against its leader, Manuel Antonio Noriega Moreno, on charges of drug trafficking. It is what some historians called the "War That Started All Wars—or at least the war that started all of Washington's post-Cold War wars." I can't express all the emotions I experience there in Panama, but I can say Glory to God. I made it back safe and alive. May God continue to bless the families of my brothers who did not.

CHAPTER 5: PTSD - POST TRAUMATIC STRESS DISORDER

Richard Gabriel, in his book No More Heroes, said, "Nations customarily measure the 'costs of war' in dollars, lost production, or the number of soldiers killed or wounded. The military establishments rarely attempt to estimate the costs of war in terms of individual human suffrage. Psychiatric breakdown remains one of the costliest items of war when expressed in human terms." War truly is hell. It is like living in a nightmare without the hope of waking up. Ever! Think of a horror movie scene where you can see the star (or a random stupid character) hears a noise outside. They look out of the window but sees nothing. So, they decide to walk outside and look around, in search of the source. The spooky music starts to play, and shadows start popping up, but instead of the person moving back to a safe place, they move further away.

Soon we see the killer's weapon of choice as the victim realizes that coming outside was a wrong choice. The music gets louder as the killer gets closer to the victim. The music stops because the victim made it to safety. They relax and breathe. Next, the high-pitched shrieks slip past your eardrum as chills run down your spine and grip your soul. You know it is a movie but, everything within you wants to escape to a safe place. Your eyes fixed, your nerves twitched with the urge to flee before the killer set their gaze on you — the victim squirms and flails as they fight for a final breath. Then, silence. It's over. The victim is deceased, scene over. The cops maul over the mutilated body wonder who could be so twisted to destroy a body in that manner. Well, war is like living in that scene with the eerie music blaring at all times. The killer is always present adrenalin continually flowing. You are personally sensitive to every shadow or sound manifesting in your personal space. You don't want to go to sleep because you know the killer has killed others and will stop at nothing to decimate you. You are always walking on pins and needles. Everything in you wants to live and return to your old life without fear of death.

Nevertheless, you feel Death is always present. When you are at war, the killer is out there somewhere, anywhere, and your job is to spot and kill them before they kill you. It is nothing you can easily forget, and if that emotional valve stays open too long, it becomes harder if not nearly impossible to shut off. This high level of stress is what many professionals consider one of the earliest symptoms of PTSD. A person returning from war exhibiting these symptoms and manifestations is a psychiatric casualty. Merriam-Webster defines Post-Traumatic Stress Disorder, commonly called PTSD as:

A psychological reaction that occurs after experiencing a highly stressing event (as wartime combat, physical violence, or a natural disaster) outside the range of typical human experience including depression, anxiety, flashbacks, recurrent nightmares, and avoidance of reminders of the event—abbreviation PTSD. PTSD is also delayed-stress disorder, delayed-stress syndrome, post-traumatic stress syndrome. Defining PTSD is an ongoing process. The description continues to become most details as we are still gaining insight into this diagnosis. Statically most soldiers who survive trauma experienced serving in combat zones being exposed to traumatic experiences return to normal given a little time. But that is not true for everyone. Some of these stress reactions don't quickly go away but may even worsen over time. These individuals are at high risk of being diagnosed as developing PTSD. An online video program called Buzzsaw says:

• Every day, at least two U.S. veterans commit suicide.

• 98% of PTSD suicidal soldiers are male.

• About 8000 veterans per year kill themselves (this number includes soldiers from the Vietnam War to the current wars in Iraq and Afghanistan.)

• These numbers exclude Suicide by Cop, accidental overdoses, alcohol poisoning, driving a car across six lanes of traffic to avoid being remembered by loved ones for killing themselves, ensuring their families can get the insurance money. Most of the veterans know if their buddies killed themselves.

• One in three returning for Iraq and Afghanistan has considered or is considering taking their own lives.

Author Richard Gabriel said the some of the symptoms of PTSD are fatigue cases, confused states, conversion hysteria, anxiety states, obsessional and compulsive states, and character disorders. Mr. Gabriel said physical and mental exhaustion is one of the earliest symptoms, including an increasingly unsociable and overly irritable, the soldier loses interest in all activities with friends and seeks to avoid any responsibility or action involving physical or mental effort. He goes on to say PTSD suffers, "often relive the experience through nightmares and flashbacks, have difficulty sleeping, and feel detached or estranged, and these symptoms can be severe enough and last long enough to impair the person's daily life significantly." The information is consistent in persons with PTSD.

A simple history of PTSD

Since the age of man fighting off an attack by saber tooth tigers, humanity has had traumatic experiences. Authors have been writing about PTSD for centuries. A few examples:

- Homer's The Iliad
- William Shakespeare's Henry IV
- Charles Dickens' A Tale of Two Cities

Initially, PTSD was called Nostalgia by Swiss military physicians in 1678, but other countries also knew it by a different name. Nostalgia defines a condition characterized "by melancholy, incessant thinking of home, disturbed sleep or insomnia, weakness, loss of appetite, anxiety, cardiac palpitations, stupor, and fever."

Around 1700 a French surgeon named Dominique Jean Larrey provided a more precise conceptualization of the disorder, which he described the disease as having three stages.

Stage 1: A heightened excitement and imagination

Stage 2: A period of fever and prominent gastrointestinal symptoms.

Stage 3: A frustration and depression.

It was over 150 years before Dorothea Dix of the United States advocated for the humane treatment of the mentally ill, prompting the U.S. Government to establish the Government Hospital for the Insane in Washington, D.C., in 1855. It was at this hospital that American military physicians began documenting the occurrence of fears and stresses related to the military duties of Civil War soldiers.

In 1871 Cardiologist Jacob Mendez Da Costa discovered what he called "soldier's heart" or "irritable heart." He observed that soldiers differed in their higher blood pressure and heart rate during the Civil War years. With the advent of modern warfare, many soldiers suffered from psychological wounds from the horrific experience. Ironically, it was believed then as some still today that soldiers who had PTSD during this time are considered weak.

Robert C. Wood, 1864 the assistant surgeon general, stated: "It is my lack of discipline, confidence, and respect that many a young soldier has become discouraged and made to feel the bitter pangs of homesickness, which is usually the precursor of more serious ailments." As the medical community continued to study combat soldiers by 1905, doctors began to call these traumatized soldiers "battle shock." Doctors continued to search for the trigger of this condition.

In World War1, psychologists believed the distress of soldiers attributed to concussions caused by the impact of shells, which disrupted the brain and cause "shell shock."

As a child, I remembered hearing people being called "Shell

shock" after returning from World War II, the Korean and Vietnam wars. They walked around in a dazed, disoriented state.

Although doctors were making progress, they realized that soldiers not exposed to exploding shells were experiencing similar symptoms. The treatment for 'shell shock' was a few days of comfort, then soldiers return to duty. The procedure was a success because 65% of shell-shocked soldiers were able to return to the front lines.

Sigmund Freud also chimed in and shared his belief in the study of 'shell shock' patients. By now, these soldiers called 'war neuroses' because some soldiers exhibited the same symptoms with being exposed to the shelling. Dr. Freud conceptualized war neuroses brought about by conflicts between a soldiers' "war egos" and "peace egos." He goes on to say that, "The war neuroses, in so far as they differ from the ordinary neuroses of peacetime through particular peculiarities, are to be regarded as traumatic neuroses, whose existence has been rendered possible or promoted through an ego-conflict...The conflict takes place between the old ego of peacetime and the new war-ego of the soldier, and it becomes acute as soon as the peace-ego is in danger of being killed through the risky undertakings of his newly formed parasitical double. The old ego protects itself from the danger to life by flight into the traumatic neurosis in defending itself against the new ego, which it recognizes as threatening its life." Ultimately Freud believed that "shell shock" was the result of emotional problems rather than the physical injury of the brain. Psychiatrists found that "weak" soldiers were predisposed to this condition, and their primary aim was to use psychiatric testing to weed out these potential psychological casualties in war.

Some military professionals questioned the legitimacy of war neuroses, stating that, "War neurosis which persists is not a creditable disease to have...as it indicates in practically every case a lack of the soldierly qualities which have distinguished the Allied Armies...no one should be permitted to glorify himself as a case of 'shell shock'".

The risk of war neuroses increased during World War II with the advent of bigger bombs and battlefield weapons, placing soldiers at higher risk of death. Despite various changes by military leaders to screen soldiers and create smaller teams, the war still took a tremendous psychological toll on soldiers.

The number of soldiers affected by war trauma was so high that psychiatrists concluded with the reality that psychological weakness had little to do with subsequent distress in combat. This revelation led to a change in terminology. The military rebranded War neuroses or combat neurosis to "combat exhaustion" or "battle fatigue," which prompted the U.S. Army to adopt the slogan, "Every man has his breaking point." The U.S. Army released a documentary entitled Shades of Gray (Not to be confused with Fifty Shaded of Gray) about what they believed to be the causes and treatment of mental illness. The documentary expressed the revelation that no soldier is immune to mental illness, and their environment played a significant role in the development of psychological problems. The new information also led to a shift in treatment. It went from just a few days of rest & relaxation to rest in safe areas, also prescribing sodium Pentothal (or other barbiturates) to some soldiers, which induce repressed battlefield experiences. Liquor became medicine to help soldiers cope, but not everyone believed that "combat exhaustion" or "battle fatigue" was an actual condition. Some leaders still thought that it was merely a case of a weak, cowardly soldier trying to get a vacation from the war on the army's dime or budget.

During World War II, President Roosevelt received thousands of letters about the incident when General Patton showed no respect for battle fatigue soldiers. General George Patton slapped two soldiers who were recuperating in a military hospital while yelling to a medical officer, "Don't admit this yellow bastard… There's nothing the matter with him. I won't have the hospitals cluttered up with these sons of bitches who haven't got the guts to fight". President Roosevelt ordered General Patton to apologize and relieved him as Commander of the Seventh Army. His command changed, but his mindset did not.

With the passing of the National Mental Health Act in 1946,

the Veteran Administration Center began to treat mental health problems in veterans. Even with all the advancements in treatment battle, fatigued soldiers to them equaled as physiologically weak or constitutionally disordered. Leaders in the field of psychological considered the cause to be biological, stating, "The psychological problems arose from pathologies in early childhood, and that psychological problems were converted into physical symptoms, manifesting themselves in such diverse diseases as ulcers, arthritis, dermatitis, and hyperthyroidism." The American Psychiatric Association went on to the creation of the first diagnostic manual known as the Diagnostic and Statistical Manual I (DSM-I).

The Vietnam War was a turning point for combat exhaustion studies. The measures taken to decrease the psychological impact of war on soldiers did not last. By the end of the conflict, new issues arose, creating an even higher number of psychologically impacted soldiers emerged. As the Vietnam War waged on, the public outcry about the legitimacy of the war led to even greater stigmatization of soldiers leading to readjustment issues. Unlike previous wars, Vietnam vets were not welcome back from the war, which facilitated ` the rise to our current understanding of PTSD. American society offered little acceptance of Vietnam veterans even years after the war. In 1969 APA members Pettera, Johnson, and Zimmer coined the term "Vietnam combat reaction." It was a term used to describe a more extreme form of combat fatigue seen mostly in soldiers nearing the end of their tours, possibly bearing long-term consequences. By the end of the Vietnam War, it became clear that many soldiers were suffering severe psychological effects as a result of their traumatic exposure. It wasn't until the American Psychiatric Association released the Diagnostic and Statistical Manual III. The term combat exhaustion became Post-Traumatic Stress Disorder. The authors of the DSM III struggled with many issues such as:

• "How severe should the trauma be?

• What types of injury could be considered causative?

• Does it make a difference if the trauma is inflicted by another human being, by accident, or by a natural disaster?

• What impact does the duration of the stressor have?

• What effect does premorbid psychiatric status have?

"Post-traumatic Stress Disorder or PTSD is a complex concept in which the criteria continue to change since 1980. According to a recent edition of the DSM-IV-TR, "PTSD can arise even as a result of a threat to the physical integrity of another, leaving room for "vicarious traumatization" or "secondary traumatic stress." That is, even individuals, such as family members or helping professionals exposed to the traumatic experiences of others, can be susceptible to developing PTSD symptoms themselves." Anyone can develop PTSD, even men of God. There was a prophet in the

Old Testament who suffered from PTSD. His name was Elijah.

PTSD: Elijah's Thorn

To some people, this may seem shocking, or even in error that the Prophet Elijah suffered from PTSD, let me assure you it is not in error. The Apostle Paul, that great man of God who wrote a third of the New Testament had a thorn in the flesh that buffeted him. In 2 Corinthians 12:6-7 Paul said,

"For if I do wish to boast I will not be foolish, for I will be speaking the truth; but I refrain from this, so that no one will credit me with more than he sees in me or hears from me. [7] Because of the surpassing greatness of the revelations, for this reason, to keep me from exalting myself, there was given me a thorn in the flesh, a messenger of Satan to torment me--to keep me from exalting myself!"

Some things bothered Paul to the point he prayed to God for relief, but the thorn in his life served a purpose, and he found resolution in God. In the New Bible Commentary, they shed light on Paul's thorn in the flesh this way, "Is there a single servant of Christ who cannot point to some thorn in the flesh visible or private, physical or psychological from which he has prayed to be released, but humble, and therefore fruitful in His service? Every believer must learn that human weakness and divine grace go hand in hand together."

The term 'thorn in your side' concerning the problems or spiritual attacks that plague God's people did not originate in the New Testament but can also trace back to the Old Testament in Numbers 33:54-55. Numbers 33:54-55 says,

"And ye shall divide the land by lot for an inheritance among your families: and to the more ye shall give the more inheritance, and to the fewer ye shall give the less inheritance: every man's inheritance shall be in the place where his lot falleth; according to the tribes of your fathers ye shall inherit, 55 But if ye will not drive out the inhabitants of the land from before you; then it shall come to pass, that those which ye let remain of them shall be pricks in your eyes, and thorns in your sides, and shall vex you in the land wherein ye dwell."

Other scriptures in the Old Testament referring to the thorns that buffeted Israel: Joshua 23:13, Ezekiel 28:24, and Hosea 2:6.

Even King David, whom the Bible called a man after God's own heart, had his share of challenges but went on to say in Psalm 34:19 that many are the afflictions of the righteous, but the Lord delivers him out of them all. As it was with King David and Paul, so it was with Elijah. The Amplified Bible describes Elijah this way in James 5:17a, "Elijah was a man with a nature like ours [with the same physical, mental, and spiritual limitations and shortcomings]," meaning he was not so spiritual that he could not have PTSD. You will see in the pages to come that he not only sufferer from PTSD, but with God's help, found a road to recovery.

CHAPTER 6: ELIJAH - SOLDIER WITH A CAUSE

"It always seems impossible until it is done." Nelson Mandela

To truly understand Elijah and the things he experienced leading up to PSTD, you must read I King chapters 16, 17, 18 & 19. I have taken the liberty to provide the most pertinent portion of the scriptures to paint a clear picture, but please read the chapters in their entirety. Let the journey begin.

I King 16: 29-33

"[29] In the thirty-eighth year of Asa king of Judah, Ahab the son of Omri became King over Israel; and Ahab the son of Omri reigned over Israel in Samaria twenty-two years. [30] Now Ahab the son of

Omri did evil in the sight of the Lord, more than all who were before him. [31] And it came to pass, as though it had been a trivial thing for him to walk in the sins of Jeroboam the son of Nebat that he took as wife Jezebel the daughter of Ethbaal, King of the Sidonians; and he went and served Baal and worshiped him. [32] Then he set up an altar for Baal in the temple of Baal, which he had built in Samaria. [33] And Ahab made a wooden image Ahab did more to provoke the Lord God of Israel to anger than all the kings of Israel who were before him."

I King 17:1

"And Elijah the Tishbite, of the inhabitants of Gilead, said to Ahab, "As the Lord God of Israel lives, before whom I stand, there shall not be dew nor rain these years, except at my word."

1 Kings 18:1-4, 7-8, 16-46 And it came to pass after many days that the word of the Lord came to Elijah, in the third year, saying, "Go, present yourself to Ahab, and I will send rain on the earth." [2] So Elijah went to present himself to Ahab; and there was a severe famine in Samaria. [3] And Ahab had called Obadiah, who was in charge of his house. (Now Obadiah feared the Lord greatly. [4] For so it was, while Jezebel massacred the prophets of the Lord, that Obadiah had taken one hundred prophets and hidden them, fifty to a cave, and had fed them with bread and water.) [5] And Ahab had said to Obadiah, "Go into the land to all the springs of water and to all the brooks; perhaps we may find grass to keep the horses

and mules alive, so that we will not have to kill any livestock."; [7] Now as Obadiah was on his way, suddenly Elijah met him; and he recognized him, and fell on his face, and said, "Is that you, my lord Elijah?" [8] And he answered him, "It is I. Go, tell your master, 'Elijah is here.'"

[16] So Obadiah went to meet Ahab, and told him; and Ahab went to meet Elijah. [17] Then it happened, when Ahab saw Elijah, that Ahab said to him, "Is that you, O troubler of Israel?" [18] And he answered, "I have not troubled Israel, but you and your father's house have, in that you have forsaken the commandments of the Lord and have followed the Baals. [19] Now therefore, send and gather all Israel to me on Mount Carmel, the four hundred and fifty prophets of Baal, and the four hundred prophets of Asherah,[a] who eat at Jezebel's table." [20] So Ahab sent for all the children of Israel, and gathered the prophets together on Mount Carmel. [21] And Elijah came to all the people, and said, "How long will you falter between two opinions? If the Lord is God, follow Him; but if Baal, follow him." But the people answered him not a word. [22] Then Elijah said to the people, "I alone am left a prophet of the Lord; but Baal's prophets are four hundred and fifty men. [23] Therefore let them give us two bulls; and let them choose one bull for themselves, cut it in pieces, and lay it on the wood, but put no fire under it; and I will prepare the other bull, and lay it on the wood, but put no fire under it. [24] Then you call on the name of your gods,

and I will call on the name of the Lord; and the God who answers by fire, He is God." So all the people answered and said, "It is well spoken." [25] Now Elijah said to the prophets of Baal, "Choose one bull for yourselves and prepare it first, for you are many; and call on the name of your god, but put no fire under it." [26] So they took the bull which was given them, and they prepared it, and called on the name of Baal from morning even till noon, saying, "O Baal, hear us!" But there was no voice; no one answered. Then they leaped about the altar which they had made.[27] And so it was, at noon, that Elijah mocked them and said, "Cry aloud, for he is a god; either he is meditating, or he is busy, or he is on a journey, or perhaps he is sleeping and must be awakened." [28] So they cried aloud, and cut themselves, as was their custom, with knives and lances, until the blood gushed out on them. [29] And when midday was past, they prophesied until the time of the offering of the evening sacrifice. But there was no voice; no one answered, no one paid attention.[30] Then Elijah said to all the people, "Come near to me." So all the people came near to him. And he repaired the altar of the Lord that was broken down. [31] And Elijah took twelve stones, according to the number of the tribes of the sons of Jacob, to whom the word of the Lord had come, saying, "Israel shall be your name." [32] Then with the stones he built an altar in the name of the Lord; and he made a trench around the altar large enough to hold two seahs of seed. [33] And he put the wood in order, cut the bull in pieces, and laid it on the wood, and said, "Fill four water pots with water, and pour it on the burnt sacrifice and on the wood." [34] Then he said, "Do it a second time," and they did it a second time; and he said, "Do it a third time," and they did it a third time. [35] So the water ran all around the altar; and he also filled the trench with water. [36] And it came to pass, at the time of the offering of the evening sacrifice, that Elijah the prophet came near and said, "Lord God of Abraham, Isaac, and Israel, let it be known this day that You are God in Israel and I am Your servant, and that I have done all these things at Your word. [37] Hear me, O Lord, hear me, that this people may know that You are the Lord God, and that You have turned their hearts back to You again." [38] Then the fire of the Lord fell and consumed the burnt sacrifice, and the wood and the stones and the dust, and it licked up the water that was in the trench. [39] Now when all the people saw it, they fell on their faces; and they said, "The Lord, He is God! The Lord, He is God!" [40] And Elijah said to them, "Seize the prophets of Baal! Do not let one of them escape!" So they seized them; and Elijah brought them down to the Brook Kishon and executed them there. [43] and said to his servant, "Go up now, look toward the sea." So he went up and looked, and said, "There is nothing." And seven times he said, "Go again." [44] Then it came to pass the seventh time, that he said, "There is a cloud, as small as a man's hand, rising out of the sea!" So he said, "Go up, say to Ahab, 'Prepare your chariot, and go down before the rain stops you.'" [45] Now it happened in the meantime that the sky became black with clouds and wind, and there was a heavy rain. So Ahab rode away and went to Jezreel. [46] Then the hand of the Lord came upon Elijah; and he girded up his loins and ran ahead of Ahab to the entrance of Jezreel. 1 Kings 19 NKJV says,

"[1] And Ahab told Jezebel all that Elijah had done, also how he had executed all the prophets with the sword. [2] Then Jezebel sent a messenger to Elijah, saying, "So let the gods do to me, and more also, if I do not make your life as the life of one of them by tomorrow about this time." [3] And when he saw that, he arose and ran for his life, and went to Beersheba, which belongs to Judah, and left his servant there. [4] But he himself went a day's journey into the wilderness, and came and sat down under a broom tree. And he prayed that he might die, and said, "It is enough! Now, Lord, take my life, for I am no better than my fathers!" [5] Then as he lay and slept under a broom tree, suddenly an angel[a] touched him, and said to him, "Arise and eat." [6] Then he looked, and there by his head was a cake baked on coals, and a jar of water. So he ate and drank, and lay down again. [7] And the angel[b] of the Lord came back the second time, and touched him, and said, "Arise and eat, because the journey is too great for you." [8] So he arose, and ate and drank; and he went in the strength of that food forty days and forty nights as far as Horeb, the mountain of God. [9] And there he went into a cave, and spent the night in that place; and behold, the word of the Lord came to him, and He said to him, "What are you doing here, Elijah?" [10] So he said, "I have been very zealous for the Lord God of hosts; for the children of Israel have forsaken Your covenant, torn down Your altars, and killed Your prophets with the sword. I alone am left; and they seek to take my life." [11] Then He said, "Go out, and stand on the mountain before the Lord." And behold, the Lord passed by, and a great and strong wind tore into the mountains and broke the rocks in pieces before the Lord, but the Lord was not in the wind; and after the wind an earthquake, but the Lord was not in the earthquake; [12] and after the earthquake a fire, but the Lord was not in the fire; and after the fire a still small voice. [13] So it was, when Elijah heard it, that he wrapped his face in his mantle and went out and stood in the entrance of the cave. Suddenly a voice came to him, and said, "What are you doing here, Elijah?" [14] And he said, "I have been very zealous for the Lord God of hosts; because the children of Israel have forsaken Your covenant, torn down Your altars, and killed Your prophets with the sword. I alone am left; and they seek to take my life." [15] Then the Lord said to him: "Go, return on your way to the Wilderness of Damascus; and when you arrive, anoint Hazael as King over Syria. [16] Also you shall anoint Jehu the son of Nimshi as King over Israel. And Elisha the son of Shaphat of Abel Meholah you shall anoint as prophet in your place. [17] It shall be that whoever escapes the sword of Hazael, Jehu will kill; and whoever escapes the sword of Jehu, Elisha will kill [18] Yet I have reserved seven thousand in Israel, all whose knees have not bowed to Baal, and every mouth that has not kissed him." [19] So he departed from there, and found Elisha the son of Shaphat, who was plowing with twelve yoke of oxen before him, and he was with the twelfth. Then Elijah passed by him and threw his mantle on him. [20] And he left the oxen and ran after Elijah, and said, "Please let me kiss my father and my mother, and then I will follow you."

I know that was a lot to take in. If you' were not familiar with the story of Elijah and Ahab, it was necessary to see how Elijah came to display the symptoms of PTSD and how God cared for him.

In summary, Elijah was a prophet of the Lord, who was sent by God to speak to a King named Ahab. Prophets in the bible did many things regarding the charge of God such as called to speak, fight, or lead as soldiers. Sometimes prophets did what they believed was best for themselves or their safety. They proclaimed the word of God, but some lead God's people into battle. This call was answered by prophets of God, such as Deborah, Gideon, Elijah, and Elisha, to name a few.

King Ahab, along with his wife Jezebel, provoked the anger of the Lord, by persuading her husband to build an altar to the false gods, forsaking God's commandments and worshipped Baal instead. As punishment for leading God's people into sin and away from a healthier way of life, Elijah proclaimed a drought in the land for three and a half years. During the three and a half years drought, Elijah hid to avoid King Ahab, who sought to kill him for proclaiming the drought. At the end of three and a half years, God sent Elijah to confront Ahab. Before allowing the rain to return, Elijah proposed to Ahab contest between himself and the King's prophets. They would build two altars to their respective gods, layout a sacrifice, and the God who consumes the sacrifice by fire is indeed God. The priests of Baal called upon their god Baal to send down fire, but there was no answer. Elijah called upon his God, and fire came down and burnt up all the offerings. The people realized the 450 prophets of Baal and Jezebel 400 priests were false, and Elijah kills them all.

War is messy

Just think of Elijah as a Rambo for God on active duty. His job was to lead God's people back to the one true God, away from the false teaching of King Ahab and his wife. The King was failing to adhere to the warning God, Elijah using the weapon of faith, deploys a drought bomb causing Ahab's kingdom to dry up for three and a half years. Ahab retaliated by sending out a kill order against Elijah. After three and a half years, Elijah surfaces to do battle. They did battle on a mountain top, and the weapons of choice were the powers of their god versus the power of Elijah's

God. Elijah wins the fight, but the war is not over. The Queen learned that Elijah slew her army of priests sent out a new kill order. Only hers was more lethal than the King. It is at this point we see Post Traumatic Stress Disorder displayed in Elijah's life.

Let's look at some of the causes, signs, and symptoms of PTSD. You may be asking yourself how a person can actively serve God, following orders from God, still subsequently be a victim of PTSD. Is it possible? Yes, it is! God also gave a compelling disclosure to help prevent some of the causes of PTSD.

In Numbers 32, God provides a promise to the nation of Israel about returning from battle guiltless because they were soldiering for him. Numbers 32:20-22 says,

"So this is a promise — if you do this thing, if you arm yourselves before the Lord for the war ... you shall return, you're coming back, and be guiltless before the Lord and before the nation." Can a person actively serving God, following orders from God, still subsequently be a victim of PTSD Yes. PTSD is complicated and goes beyond guilt.

One thing I would like to share from my brief combat experience as compared to the current six to eighteen months deployments. A necessary part of operating in a war zone is the ability to disconnect from our civilian home life and becoming survival-focused. If you have never served in a war zone, this is necessary for a soldier's survival. We must shut off our personal lives in a split second or moments notices to protect and serve our coharts and country. It is our connections with friends and family's that keep us civil. Civility tends to fly out of the window when amid bullets, bombs, and chaos. As time progresses and the longer we stay away from civility, war tends to unravel a soldier's minds in a way it becomes harder to reconnect with our loves due to the experiences, guilt, and shames war produces. God understands and has forgiven us, but we must forgive ourselves.

I would like to borrow a quote from George Orwell in his book *Why I Write*:

"As I write, highly civilized human beings are flying overhead, trying to kill me. They do not feel any enmity against me as an individual nor against them. They are 'only doing their duty,' as the saying goes. Most of them, I have no doubt, are kind-hearted law-abiding men who would never dream of murdering private life. On the other hand, if one of them succeeds in blowing me to pieces with a well-placed bomb, he will never sleep any the worse for it. He is serving his country, which has the power to absolve him from evil."

His sentiments expressed exactly my views as well about wartime. In terms of the bible, God has also freed our conscience of guilt. God pronounced soldiers fighting to protect their country's guiltless. Forgiveness is a powerful gift. Guilt is a killer if not adequately confronted.

War is messy

It's full of things so horrific that it causes a person to rethink their entire existence. In Panama, I faced my peers, who mistakenly thought I was an enemy combatant. Viewing a massive number of dead bodies stacked on the side of the road left me dealing with a multitude of emotions. Years after leaving the military, I found myself sitting on my couch in Texas crying, trying to understand what we had done to that country after watching a documentary on Operation Just Cause. Tears of guilt were tearing me apart, but guilt rarely travels alone. It usually come with shame.

Shame is not a new issue that trouble humankind. It is one of the first open emotions God had to address with humanity. Shame first displayed in the bible, Genesis three, when Adam and Eve realized they were naked and hid.

Shame is a fear of being disconnected from others. Adam knew that partaking of the fruit changed his relationship with God because the glory of God no longer shone upon them, as we saw in an earlier chapter. Shame is the same emotion that grips some soldiers returning from war. Many are afraid their civilian loved ones won't understand what we may have seen, experienced, or partake in the activities. In the Old Testament, God, through the mouth of the prophets, gave orders to kill everyone, including men, women, children, and animals. The orders included babies, and I'm sure the soldiers of the bible experienced the same as soldiers returning from Vietnam. Soldiers who are today returning from the war are called "babies' killers" and "murders."

Guilt and shame don't discriminate.

For many, guilt and shame are the same emotions, but they are different. Dr. Breme' Brown (a leading researcher on shame) said in her TED talk, "Shame is not guilt. Shame is a focus on self. Guilt is a focus behavior. Shame says I am bad; guilt is I did something bad. Guilt says I'm sorry I made a mistake; shame says I sorry I am a mistake. Shame correlates with addiction, depression, aggression, bullying, suicide, and eating disorders. Guilt inversely correlated with these things."

War tends to leave people feeling unworthy of love from themselves, others, and God. It leaves soldiers feeling as if this world is so screwed up. Why are people so bent on destroying the lives of others for their cause? Soldiers are experiencing the misery of war, battling with unanswered questions while daily living on the edge of life and deaths, find it hard to experience hope and trust in people who shared the same or similar experiences. Partaking of war leaves many feelings unworthy to reconnect with the civilian world. God foresaw this issue and declared the soldiers who honestly fought to protect their nation's worth of the love from Him and others. He declares us guiltless of war issues, according to Numbers 32:20-22.

Dr. Brown says we cannot numb guilt and shame without numbing the other emotions. The key to becoming free from guilt is to become vulnerable.

Some view vulnerability for military soldiers as negative and weak, but to be vulnerable requires the courage to expose our inner secrets to someone else. Expose the secrets of guilt and shames tends to cause them to disappear over time. The concern for many soldiers is that as they expose the things (memories of war), they fear others will declare them unworthy of their love or even judge them. You will be amazed at the love you could receive from your loved one whom you allow into the painful space. Just accept the grace and love of God to fill that hurt and shame. As I said before, war is messy, ugly, and nasty. It leads to physical death for some and an emotional end for others. Jesus made it plain that no greater love than a man who is willing to give his life for a friend.

Jesus' disciples thought of Him as a military leader coming to over through the Roman army, which had occupied their home-land. He led like a commander, followed the orders of God like a good soldier, and paid the ultimate price for his beliefs, not did not give up his followers so that he would not die alone. He stayed true to his mission until death so that others may live. Jesus, the expressed image of God's Love, understands a soldier's sacrifice and how precious it is to God. Some may never completely understand, but God does.

Sadly, many of the greatest critics of war enjoy the freedom we as soldiers fought for while being unwilling to make the sacrifice themselves. President Theodore Roosevelt said in his speech Citizenship in A Republic that,

"It is not the critic who counts; not the man who points out how the strong man stumbles, or where the doer of deeds could have done them better. The credit belongs to the man who is actually in the arena, whose face is marred by dust and sweat and blood; who strives valiantly; who errs, who comes short again and again, because there is no effort without error and shortcoming; but who does strive to do the deeds; who knows great enthusiasms, the great devotions; who spends himself in a worthy cause; who at the best knows, in the end, the triumph of high achievement, and who at the worst, if he fails, at least fails while daring greatly, so that his place shall never be with those cold and timid souls who neither know victory nor defeat."

It is okay for you to talk out your pains via friends or adequate professional counseling. The message is ongoing in the bible. Here are a few supporting scriptures:

Proverbs 15:22, "Without counsel, plans fail, but with many advisers, they succeed."

Proverbs 20:5 ESV, "The purpose in a man's heart is like deep water, but a man of understanding will draw it out."

John 16:13 ESV, "When the Spirit of truth comes, he will guide you into all the truth, for he will not speak on his own authority, but whatever he hears he will speak, and he will declare to you the things that are to come."

Proverbs 12:18 ESV, "There is one whose rash words are like sword thrusts, but the tongue of the wise brings healing."

2 Timothy 3:16-17 ESV, "All Scripture is breathed out by God and profitable for teaching, for reproof, for correction, and for training in righteousness, that the man of God may be competent, equipped for every good work." Galatians 6:2 ESV

Galatians 6:2 ESV, "Bear one another's burdens, and so fulfill the law of Christ." Proverbs 1:1-3 ESV

Proverbs 1:1-3 ESV, "The proverbs of Solomon, son of David, king of Israel: To know wisdom and instruction, to understand words of insight, to receive instruction in wise dealing, in righteousness, justice, and equity;"

Romans 15:14 ESV, "I myself am satisfied about you, my brothers, that you yourselves are full of goodness, filled with all knowledge and able to instruct one another."

1 Peter 5:7 ESV, "Casting all your anxieties on him because he cares for you."

Proverbs 27:9 ESV, "Oil and perfume make the heart glad, and the sweetness of a friend comes from his earnest counsel." Proverbs 11:14 ESV

Proverbs 11:14 ESV, "Where there is no guidance, a people falls, but in an abundance of counselors there is safety." Proverbs 11:13-15 ESV

Proverbs 11:13-15 ESV, "Humble yourselves, therefore, under the mighty hand of God so that at the proper time he may exalt you." 1 Peter 5:6

1 Peter 5:6, "God opposes the proud but gives grace to the humble."

James 4:6, "…you were made sorrowful to the point of repentance; for you were made sorrowful according to the will of God… For the sorrow that is according to the will of God produces a repentance without regret, leading to salvation…"

2 Corinthians 7:9-10, " Now I rejoice, not that ye were made sorry, but that ye sorrowed to repentance: for ye were made sorry after a godly manner, that ye might receive damage by us in nothing. [10] For godly sorrow worketh repentance to salvation not to be repented of: but the sorrow of the world worketh death."

CHAPTER 7: ELIJAH'S PTSD – SYMPTONS AND BEHAVIORS

"I signed up to protect this country. I do not choose the wars." Chris Kyle

The Prophet Elijah is a very prominent figure throughout the Bible. The Apostle James 5:17-18 NIV says, "Elijah was a human being, even as we are. He prayed earnestly that it would not rain, and it did not rain on the land for three and a half years. [18] Again he prayed, and the heavens gave rain, and the earth produced its crops."

Guilt plays a significant role in PTSD (although there also physical contributing factors) God's promise plays a role in the healing process. The need for God to provide a promise of guilt-less-ness means that some soldiers will experience guilt from the things they see, committed, encounter, and endured in war.

As previously stated, leaders need to understand that as the modernization of the weapons of our warfare increases, so does the trauma of soldiers.

As James said, Elijah was a prophet, but he was also a man like every other soldier.

Being human, he was susceptible to and experienced PTSD, just like soldiers today. Merriam-Webster defines PTSD as a psychological reaction that occurs after experiencing a highly stressing event (as wartime combat, physical violence, or a natural disaster) outside the range of normal human experience. It's characterized by depression, anxiety, flashbacks, recurrent nightmares, and avoidance of reminders of the event.

First king 18:22 has the first indication that Elijah had PTSD, which says, "Elijah said to the people, "I alone am left a prophet of the Lord; but Baal's prophets are four hundred and fifty men." He makes this statement after coming out of three and a half years of hiding.

But we read in an earlier verse, "Now as Obadiah was on his way, suddenly Elijah met him; and he recognized him, and fell on his face, and said, "Is that you, my lord Elijah?" Obadiah is a minor prophet in the Old Testament. The Minor Prophets, "minor" because their books are shorter than the "Major Prophets," but they are of equal importance to the people of God as the Major Prophets are in the writings of the Major Prophets. It appears that he felt he was the only soldier committed to the call of God before going into this battle. Later after he expressed this feeling of being alone to God, God reveals to him that He had seven thousand saints who had not bowed a knee nor followed the false gods of Ahab and Jezebel.

Dr. Guy Winch Ph.D. on the Psychology Today website said, "A new study found many returning veterans, POWs, and others with severe PTSD suffer from a unique kind of loneliness, one that begins only once they are again surrounded by family and loved ones." He goes on to say that, "despite the best efforts and intentions of those around them, they felt like aliens in their communities, strangers in a familiar land. They went through the motions of "ordinary" life but did so with a marked sense of unreality." Elijah's three years of hiding had left him feeling like a "strangers in a familiar land."

He encountered a fellow man of God but still felt alone. Before the big showdown, Elijah showed no signs of loneliness, but after the encounter, something had changed. Elijah loneliness was just the beginning sign of PTSD, but the confirmation came after the showdown.

After the big showdown in 1 King 18: 40, Elijah said to the crowd, "Seize the prophets of Baal! Do not let one of them escape!" So, they seized them; and Elijah brought them down to the Brook Kishon and executed them there." Elijah played a significant role in killing 850 false prophets and priests (up close and personal), meaning he was the executioner. Lieutenant Colonel Dave Grossman said in his book On Killing about close range kills, "At this range, the screams and cries of the enemy can be heard, adding greatly to the extent of the trauma experienced by the killer." Close kills are more traumatic then long-range kills. During long-range kills, the killer could not directly see the person face or hear the person dying.

At close range, there is no doubt.

Lieutenant Colonel Dave Grossman goes on to say, "At close range, the euphoria stage, although brief, fleeting, and not often mentioned, still appears to be experienced in some form by most soldiers. Upon being asked, most of the combat veterans whom I have interviewed will admit to having experienced a brief feeling of elation upon succeeding in killing the enemy."

This same euphoric behavior is present in Elijah after his successful great showdown. Author Gene Getz said in his book, Men of Character: Elijah: Remaining steadfast through Uncertainty, "Elijah's experiences illustrate this point both symbolically and literally. Ironically, his "emotional highs" took place on the top of Mount Carmel. Imagine the excitement and joy that must have flooded his soul when God responded to his prayers and sent fire from heaven. For three and a half years, he had been waiting for this moment. Like all of us, when Elijah experienced this incredible emotional high, he was also destined to experience an intense emotional low." He successfully killed the enemy. He felt God was with him.

It was a change from the man who said he alone was standing for God. While he was on this emotional and euphoria high, Elijah found the strength to outrun Ahab's chariot. He, as an older man, ran twenty miles and arrived before the king's horses.

Elijah behavior was consistent with that of a PTSD patient. From a very excited high of victory, he crashed to a very low despondency at the words of Jezebel. It was after Jezebel threat he became consumed by depression leading to suicidal thoughts. 1 King 19:1-2 says,

"And Ahab told Jezebel all that Elijah had done, also how he had executed all the prophets with the sword. [2] Then Jezebel sent a messenger to Elijah, saying, "So let the gods do to me, and more also, if I do not make your life as the life of one of them by tomorrow about this time."

She planned to torture and executed him for killing her prophets. This man who was might man of God. He is the same man referenced in Matthew 16:14 when Jesus asked his disciples, "Who do people say the Son of Man is?" [14] They replied, "Some say John the Baptist; others say, Elijah." Elijah is the same man who became depressed.

The Diagnostic and Statistical Manual (DSM II) provided the criteria for PTSD. The first two listed as criterion "A" defines Elijah's actions and explains his reaction to the interaction between Ahab, Jezebel, and his later conversation with God. Criterion A was established on the premise if a person face exposure to a traumatic event in which both of the following have been present such as:

 The person has experienced, witnessed, or been confronted with an event or events that involve actual or threatened death or serious injury, or a threat to the physical integrity of oneself or others.

The person's response involved intense fear, helplessness, or horror.

Based on these two comparisons alone, Elijah was not just depressed. He had PTSD. Most theologian agree that Elijah's suffer with depression, but looking at his behavior next to the DSM, he experiences are a clear example of what thousands of soldiers experience every day. In a later chapter, we address God prescription for Elijah's PTSD. God lovingly and caringly help Elijah return to work and he became an active citizen for the remainder of his time on earth. I'll also show God's methods are being applied today to help people living with PTSD. War often involves death at the hands of another. The challenge many face is distinguishing why they terminated a life. Was their combat service deemed killing or murder? Healing rest is the answer to this question. In the next chapter, we will look at both to understand the difference. The answer will free the heart and mind!

CHAPTER 8: DIFFERENCE BETWEEN KILLING & MURDER

"A lie can travel half way around the world while the truth is putting on its shoes." Mark Twain

---

I can remember watching the movie Ten Commandments and being mesmerized by actor Charlton Heston playing Moses, he stood on that mountain top and lightning struck the two tables. As the lightning hit the two perfectly flat stone tablets, the ten Commandments appeared. The lightning was symbolic of the finger of God writing the Ten Commandments. Since then, the Ten Commandments have been the butt of many jokes and bases of many stern corrections. Jokes like, "Who was the worse sinner in the Bible? Moses because he broke all Ten Commandments at one time. Ha! Ha! Ha!"

There are a significant number of people who still don't understand the 10 Commandments.

Here are a few commonly asked questions:

What is the purpose of the Ten Commandments?

Why did God give them to Moses?

Are they still for us today?

First, I'll answer the question what are the Ten Commandments? Here they are:

And God spoke these words in Exodus 20, saying,

"[2] I am the Lord thy God, which have brought thee out of the land of Egypt, out of the house of bondage.[3] Thou shalt have no other gods before me.[4] Thou shalt not make unto thee any graven image, or any likeness of anything that is in heaven above, or that is in the earth beneath, or that is in the water under the earth.[5] Thou shalt not bow down thyself to them, nor serve them: for I the Lord thy God am a jealous God, visiting the iniquity of the fathers upon the children unto the third and fourth generation of them that hate me; [6] And shewing mercy unto thousands of them that love me, and keep my commandments.[7] Thou shalt not take the name of the Lord thy God in vain; for the Lord will not hold him guiltless that taketh his name in vain.

[8] Remember the Sabbath day, to keep it holy.[9] Six days shalt thou

labour, and do all thy work:[10] But the seventh day is the Sabbath of the Lord thy God: in it thou shalt not do any work, thou, nor thy son, nor thy daughter, thy manservant, nor thy maidservant, nor thy cattle, nor thy stranger that is within thy gates:[11] For in six days the Lord made heaven and earth, the sea, and all that in them is, and rested the seventh day: wherefore the Lord blessed the Sabbath day, and hallowed it.[12] Honour thy father and thy mother: that thy days may be long upon the land which the Lord thy God giveth thee.[13] Thou shalt not kill. [14] Thou shalt not commit adultery[15] Thou shalt not steal.[16] Thou shalt not bear false witness against thy neighbour.

[17] Thou shalt not covet thy neighbour's house, thou shalt not covet thy neighbour's wife, nor his manservant, nor his maidservant, nor his ox, nor his ass, nor anything that is thy neighbour's."

For years I've heard people reject the gospel because they feel the bible tries to keep people from enjoying life. Nothing could be further from the truth. Jesus died so that we may live a healthy and abundant life. But to live an abundant live we must have guidelines to make this happen. How do I know? Judges 17:6b said, "Every man did that which was right in his own eyes." That was life after Adam sinned. Man operated conscious free until God gave Moses the Ten Commandments. Without the Commandments, people lived as it was written by the Apostle Paul who describes the lifestyle of people without the Laws of God:

Roman 1: 18-32 NKJV says,

"For the wrath of God is revealed from heaven against all ungodliness and unrighteousness of men, who suppress the truth in unrighteousness, [19] because what may be known of God is manifest in them, for God has shown it to them. [20] For since the creation of the world His invisible attributes are clearly seen, being understood by the things that are made, even His eternal power and Godhead, so that they are without excuse, [21] because, although they knew God, they did not glorify Him as God, nor were thankful, but became futile in their thoughts, and their foolish hearts were darkened. [22] Professing to be wise, they became fools, [23] and changed the glory of the incorruptible God into an image made like corruptible man—and birds and four-footed animals and creeping things. [24] Therefore God also gave them up to uncleanness, in the lusts of their hearts, to dishonor their bodies among themselves, [25] who exchanged the truth of God for the lie, and worshiped and served the creature rather than the Creator, who is blessed forever. Amen.[26] For this reason God gave them up to vile passions. For even their women exchanged the natural use for what is against nature. [27] Likewise also the men, leaving the natural use of the woman, burned in their lust for one another, men with men committing what is shameful, and receiving in themselves the penalty of their error which was due. [28] And even as they did not like to retain God in their knowledge, God gave them over to a debased mind, to do those things which are not fitting; [29] being filled with all unrighteousness, sexual immorality, wickedness, covetousness, maliciousness; full of envy, murder, strife, deceit, evil-mindedness; they are whisperers, [30] backbiters, haters of God, violent, proud, boasters, inventors of evil things, disobedient to parents, [31] undiscerning, untrustworthy, unloving, unforgiving, unmerciful; [32] who, knowing the righteous judgment of God, that those who practice such things are deserving of death, not only do the same but also approve of those who practice them."

Man lived without the law and even live that way intermittently until the fulfilled promise of a messiah arrived to reverse the curse of sin.

The Apostle Paul went on to say in Romans 5:12-13 said,

"Wherefore, as by one man sin entered into the world, and death by sin; and so death passed upon all men, for that all have sinned: [13] For until the law sin was in the world: but sin is not imputed when there is no law."

The reason sin entered the world was God gave Adam one law and he broke it. Law of sin also brought with it a consequence called death. Adam being the firstborn of man (as discussed in the previous chapter) sin spread thought his seed to every man which was born of a woman. With sin, death was inevitably to every man. Even with sin in mankind's life, it was not that man did not have an inward compass to teach them right from wrong, but man did not have an outward sign to provide consistent guidance for everyone to see and adhere for equitable expectation and fair treatment for all. Noah is an example of a man who chose right-eousness over self without the law.

After sin enter the world man went against their conscience and broke of the laws of whatever government they were living under. Man was out of control and did what was right in there on eyes. It was for this reason that God flooded the world. It's was not until the Ten Commandments came along that man received the rules for all to follow. God's original intent was to allow Israel to be a picture of a healthy nation. The other nations would see Israel equal treatment of one another while prospering and pursue God.

Sin also separate man from God. When Adam sinned his relationship with God changed. He saw the world and himself differently. The physical environment around him did not change but his thoughts about his physical environment converted from a godly purposeful environment to Satan's perverted view of God's creation. Deciding which perspective to follow rather God's or Satan is an inward conflict man struggles with daily.

In his book Believe in the God Who Believes in You: The Ten Commandments: A Divine Design for Dignity, Dr. Robert H. Schuller said,

"Each of the ten rules is a command meant to protect us from shame; preserve our self-respect and point us to a positive pride that will let us lift our heads, poised to praise and worship The Creator!"

The Apostle Paul when talking to the Galatians explains the law and the commandments in Galatians 3:19-22 AMP says,

"[19] Why, then, the Law [what was its purpose]? It was added [after the promise to Abraham, to reveal to people their guilt] because of transgressions [that is, to make people conscious of the sinfulness of sin], and [the Law] was ordained through angels and delivered to Israel by the hand of a mediator [Moses, the mediator between God and Israel, to be in effect] until the seed would come to whom the promise had been made. [20] Now the mediator or go-between [in a transaction] is not [needed] for just one party; whereas God is only one [and was the only One giving the promise to Abraham, but the Law was a contract between two, God and Israel; its validity depended on both]. [21] Is the Law then contrary to the promises of God? Certainly not! For if a system of law had been given which could impart life, then righteousness (right standing with God) would actually have been based on law. [22] But the Scripture has imprisoned everyone [everything—the entire world] under sin, so that [the inheritance, the blessing of salvation] which was promised through faith in Jesus Christ might be given to those who believe [in Him and acknowledge Him as God's precious Son]."

Even though Christ is the fulfillment of the promise, He said in Matthew 5:16-17

"Let your light so shine before men, that they may see your good works, and glorify your Father which is in heaven. Think not that I am come to destroy the law, or the prophets: I am not come to destroy, but to fulfill."

The Commandments is still providing excellent guidance as we grow in Christ. Although the Ten Commandments are equal in their objective to help us see sin, I would like to focus on the sixth Commandment (You shall not murder) as it very often misunderstood and incorrectly applied.

People use sixth Commandment to judge soldiers. The act of using the six commandments to condemn veterans is one that genuinely needs to be corrected.

For year as a young Christian I'd wondered about what appeared to be a contradiction in the word of God. God said in the sixth commandment "Thou shall not kill." If we are not supposed to kill, then why did God punish Cain for killing Able and later sent Israel out to war against their enemies to take possession of the promised land?

Many of the biblical battles ended with bloodshed and death. It is for this reason we needed to study and not just read the bible. Second Timothy 2:15 tells us to "Study to shew thyself approved unto God, a workman that needeth not to be ashamed, rightly dividing the word of truth."

So why is "Thou shall not kill" in the Ten Commandments?" It is there because it is necessary to help man see that it is wrong to kill. The confusion come when reading the King James Bible and not studying the bible but taking it all in the literal sense. The King James Version says, "Thou shalt not kill," which leaves room to misinterpret the verse. It would be a blatant disregard for His own word if God intended the meaning of "Thou shalt not kill" was just that, "no killing." God would not violate His Commandment in Deuteronomy 20, clearly endorsing the bloodletting done by the nation of Israel. As a Christian and Theologian, I know that God will never break His own commandments. King David said in Psalm 138:2,

"I will worship toward thy holy temple and praise thy name for thy lovingkindness and for thy truth: for thou hast magnified thy word above all thy name."

Numbers 23:19 says, "God is not man that he should lie; neither the son of man that he should repent: hath he said, and shall he not do it? Or hath he spoken, and shall he not make it good?"

So now the question is, "If God would never break his own his commandment, how can the bible explain God sending Israel to war and not violate this commandment?" I am glad you asked! The answer is found in looking at the original words used when the commandments were given to Moses. King James Version of the scripture says that "thou shall not kill" but the original translation says, "thou shall not commit murder". To get a clearer understand of the difference between "murder" and "killing" we need to look at the original word used. Both the Hebrew and Greek have particular terms for killing and murder. The Hebrew and Greek words for murder are "ratsakh" and "phoneuo. These words also cover deaths due to carelessness or neglect. The Hebrew root for Ratsakh is R-Tz-Ch is most commonly used to describe a murderer who kills pre-meditated or with malice. In English terms R-Tz-Ch would be murder in the first or at least the second degree. By First-degree murder, I'm referring to pre-meditated murder and Second-degree murder, meaning an intentional murder in the spur-of-the-moment, regardless if it was deliberate or planned.

The Hebrew and Greek word for killing are "muwth" and "apokteinō," which means "to cause to die" and used to describe killing during wartime.

The Hebrew root words for taking a human life other than murder are M-O-T and H-R-G. H-R-G is more commonly used to describe the taking of life in a non-criminal context, sometimes referred to as a righteous killing, but also refers to killing in self-defense or when defending the innocent. When soldiers are doing their jobs in the right manner, God sees their actions as muwth and apokteinō. Most soldiers must kill in self-defense or when defending the innocent, such as the people back home whom we pledge to defend and protect. It to this cause that God made the promise in Numbers 32:20-22 saying,

"So this is a promise — if you do this thing, if you arm yourselves before the Lord for the war ... you shall return, you're coming back, and be guiltless before the Lord and before the nation." It is a sacrifice that many soldiers make or have made. Jesus said, "No greater love than this that a man should lay down his life for a friend."

With the explanation of the difference between murder and killing, taking another person's life was never a part of God's original plan for man. We must understand the reason for killing, especially if committed in a violent act towards another human being.

Man, view murder as the physical act of taking another person's life, but how does God view Murder? To God, murder is not just a physical act, but it is a condition of one person's heart towards another. One writer said that "God defines murder as any thought or feeling of deep-seated hatred or malice against another person." We see the act of murder, but to God, it is more than just a physical action that constitutes murder. 1 John 3:15 tells us that "everyone who hates his brother is a murderer, and you know that no murderer has eternal life abiding in him."

What a difference in views. I have read that scripture on numerous occasions, but I did not think of it as such a severe offense. When we harbor hatred in our hearts for another, we have murdered in God's eyes.

Man must avoid outward disdain towards another person because God looks upon the heart for the truth. God made man to live in harmony with Himself and other human beings. The peace we once knew changed when sin entered the picture. Emotions like anger, jealousy, pride and hatred can fuel man's evil binge towards life-ending aggression.

In conclusion, murder is wrong, but this is not the word God used in the Sixth Commandment. The Sixth Commandment originally stated, "thou shall not commit murder," meaning murderer who kill pre-meditated or with malice. If you terminated a life or lives of another in the context of war, please don't condemn yourself because God does not condemn you.

In the next chapter, we will explore the heart of God as we look at a soldier who both killed and murdered.

The love of God is far more potent than the pains of war. Amen!

CHAPTER 9: KING DAVID – KILLER AND MURDERER

The life of David is one of the best document histories of one person's life in the Bible. I want to be thorough in this chapter with hopes you will be able to relate to David, his story, and the grace from God he received that we as believers and all need in our lives. Throughout this chapter, you'll see David as a soldier killing (muwth) for a godly cause, but at times you will see him taking a life for selfish reason, also known as murder(ratsakh). I included the back story on Bathsheba and Uriah, her first husband because they played a significant role in

King David's choices. In Matthew 1:6, AMP says, "Jesse, the father of King David, King David the father of Solomon, whose mother had been the wife of Uriah." Bathsheba and Uriah were the other parties involved in the murder just to show the heart of David and the evil plot behind his actions. Finally, I will show you the heart of God. I cannot say enough about the grace of God. Accessing God's grace is simple, but we must choose to embrace it!

King David.

The story of David, in general, is considered by many scholars to be, artistically, the best biblical narrative due to the amount of speech and dialogue it covers. The Bible, in general, tends to lean towards avoiding formal character portraits, but the characters (David, Bathsheba, and Uriah) come aesthetically alive through their speech. The writers comprehensively covered David's life from the time of his childhood to his death, exploring even his state of mind as revealed in the Psalms.

David was the eighth and youngest son of Jesse from the tribe of Judah and direct descendent of Ruth the Moabite. God sent the prophet Samuel to single David out and anoint him the next King after King Saul. David first come into our view as a young shepherd boy in Bethlehem. In 1 Samuel 16, we meet David.

1 Samuel 16 says:

"And the Lord said unto Samuel, How long wilt thou mourn for Saul, seeing I have rejected him from reigning over Israel? fill thine horn with oil, and go, I will send thee to Jesse the Bethlehemite: for I have provided me a king among his sons. ^{2} And Samuel said, How can I go? if Saul hear it, he will kill me. And the Lord said, Take an heifer with thee, and say, I am come to sacrifice to the Lord. ^{3} And call Jesse to the sacrifice, and I will shew thee what thou shalt do: and thou shalt anoint unto me him whom I name unto thee. ^{4} And Samuel did that which the Lord spake, …^{5} And he sanctified Jesse and his sons, and called them to the sacrifice. ^{6} And it came to pass, when they were come, that he looked on Eliab, and said, surely the Lord's anointed is before him.

It is interesting to me that God had already searched out the heart of the next King before the prophet began his search. 1 Corinthians 2:9 says,

 "But as it is written, Eye hath not seen, nor ear heard, neither have entered into the heart of man, the things which God hath prepared for them that love him."

Neither Samuel nor David knew the plan God had in mind for the future king.

Look at the criteria God used while searching for his King:

"^{7} But the Lord said unto Samuel, Look not on his countenance, or on the height of his stature; because I have refused him: for the Lord seeth not as man seeth; for man looketh on the outward appearance, but the Lord looketh on the heart. ^{10} Again, Jesse made seven of his sons to pass before Samuel. And Samuel said unto

Jesse, The Lord hath not chosen these. [11] And Samuel said unto Jesse, Are here all thy children? And he said, There remaineth yet the youngest, and, behold, he keepeth the sheep. And Samuel said unto Jesse, Send and fetch him: for we will not sit down till he come hither. [12] … Now he was ruddy, and withal of a beautiful countenance, and goodly to look to. And the Lord said, Arise, anoint him: for this is he. [14] But the Spirit of the Lord departed from Saul, and an evil spirit from the Lord troubled him. [16] Let our lord now command thy servants, which are before thee, to seek out a man, who is a cunning player on an harp: and it shall come to pass, when the evil spirit from God is upon thee, that he shall play with his hand, and thou shalt be well. [17] And Saul said unto his servants, provide me now a man that can play well, and bring him to me. [18] Then answered one of the servants, and said, Behold, I have seen a son of Jesse the Bethlehemite, that is cunning in playing, and a mighty valiant man, and a man of war, and prudent in matters, and a comely person, and the Lord is with him."

After being anointed, David returned to his sheep in the field. One day Jesse sent David to take his brother lunch. Arriving at the camp, David found the army of Israel cowering in fear for 40 days from a skilled nine-foot bronze armored Philistine giant called Goliath of Gath. Author Gene Getz tells the story of David and Goliath in his book Men of Character: David: Seeking God Faithfulness like this,

"Every day, twice a day, for forty days, the huge Philistine descended to the valley floor and shouted up to the children of Israel, challenging someone to come and fight him. His words were clear and crisp—and very foreboding to Israel: "Why do you come out to draw up in battle array? Am I not the Philistine and you servants of Saul? Choose a man for yourselves and let him come down to me. If he can fight with me and kill me, then we will become your servants; but if I prevail against him and kill him, then you shall become our servants and serve us" [vv. 8-9]. The results were devastating. "When Saul and all Israel heard these words of the Philistine, they were dismayed and greatly afraid" [v. 11]. There wasn't a man in the army of Israel who dared to accept the challenge. It would be suicide! Even their leader, Saul—the tallest of them all—was paralyzed with fear."

David immediately volunteered to become a soldier in Israel's army. The shepherd boy David made a slingshot with only a stick and a few stones. Goliath's was caught off-guard by this little shepherd boy. David approaching him with his shepherd garb, staff, and with a small sling in his hand, must have caught Goliath off-guard. Goliath understood brute strength and the use of swords, spears, or javelins, but this was a different kind of enemy. David approach may have been the first example of guerrilla warfare tactics. Goliath could defeat a man with a shield and spear, but a boy with a big mouth, a lot of confidence and a simple weapon as a slingshot, how do you fight? David, armed with his slingshot and courage, confronted the giant, invoked God's name, and killed the Goliath. The stone hit Goliath in the forehead and sunk in. David cut his head off.

After David's victory over Goliath, Saul took David on as commander of his troops. David continue to grow as a soldier. David number of kills as a soldier exceeded that of King Saul to the point that the people began to sing songs about him. 1 Samuel 18:5-7 NKJV says,

"So David went out wherever Saul sent him, and behaved wisely. And Saul set him over the men of war, and he was accepted in the sight of all the people and also in the sight of Saul's servants. [6] Now it had happened as they were coming home, when David was returning from the slaughter of the Philistine, that the women had come out of all the cities of Israel, singing and dancing, to meet King Saul, with tambourines, with joy, and with musical instruments. [7] So the women sang as they danced, and said: "Saul has slain his thousands, And David his ten thousand.".

This scripture is a perfect example of the Hebrew word and the root word for killing. Muwth and H-R-G, which means "to cause to die," also used for killing during wartime. Soldiers have no age. Some soldiers volunteer while others are select by force. David, as a soldier, had to H-R-G or kill. He had to terminate the lives of Israel's enemies known as a righteous kill. David killing in self-defense or defending of God's chosen people. It is for this reason neither God nor King Saul charged David with murder as a soldier. Citizen often praise their military leaders just as we praise American generals like George Washington, Robert E. Lee, Ulysses S. Grant, Douglas MacArthur, General Powell, or General Norman Schwarzkopf. These men killed as soldiers, but they also like soldiers today carried battles scars so the rest of the nation (Mothers, fathers, sisters, brothers, other family members, neighbors, friends, etc..) would not have too. For this cause are heroes for defending our way of life even if it led some to the grave. Also, we must continue to fight, encourage, and support our troops. War does not come without death, but God allows us to cast the weight of battle on him and not on our conscience. It is for this reason that David was not guilty of breaking the sixth commandment when he slew Goliath. On the contrary, people celebrated David for keeping the fifth commandment to Honoring thy mother and father by protecting them. In J. S Parks book The Life of King David: How God Works through Ordinary Outcasts and Extraordinary Sinners, the author said that after slinging a single stone and taking the life of Goliath, everything in David's life changed. Mr. Parks went on to say, David became a "rock-star overnight, and he plunges into a swirling spiral of fame, gossip, pop songs, envy, marriage, and murder until he's running for his very life."

David was successful in battle against the Philistines, causing Saul to be jealousy of him. Saul tried to kill David by throwing a spear at him. Saul later promised Jonathan his son, he would not try to kill David, and so he returned to the King's service. Saul broke his promise and attempted to kill David a second time, but Michal (David's wife and Saul's daughter) helped David escape to the prophet Samuel in Ramah.

Saul continually pursued him, nearly catching him a few times. David then continued his flight from Saul. David found refuge. During his escape, he gained the support of 600 men, and he and his soldiers traveled from city to city. Of the 600 men, David had a group of 30 plus men who were close to him. Here is where we discover that Uriah (Bathsheba's husband) was no stranger to King David.

•	1 Chronicles 11:10 & 11:41: These also are the chief of the mighty men whom David had, who strengthened themselves with him in his kingdom, and with all Israel, to make him king, according to the word of the LORD concerning Israel ... [41:] Uriah the Hittite

•	2 Samuel 23:8 & 23:39: These be the names of the mighty men whom David had: [39:] Uriah the Hittite: thirty and seven in all.

Eventually, David became the king of Judah. One day Saul and Jonathan were killed while fighting with the Philistines on Mt. Gilboa. David was 30 years old at the time and had ruled over

Judah for seven years and six months when he made a pact, which allowed him to unite the two kingdoms, and he ruled over all of Israel.

Bathsheba

Here is where Bathsheba enters the story. 2 Samuel 11:1-4 said:

"And it came to pass, after the year was expired, at the time when kings go forth to battle, that David sent Joab, and his servants with him, and all Israel; and they destroyed the children of Ammon, and besieged Rabbah. But David tarried still at Jerusalem. [2,] And it came to pass in an evening tide, that David arose from off his bed, and walked upon the roof of the king's house: and from the roof he saw a woman washing herself; and the woman was very beautiful to look upon.[3] And David sent and enquired after the woman. And one said, Is not this Bathsheba, the daughter of Eliam, the wife of Uriah the Hittite?[4] And David sent messengers, and took her; and she came in unto him, and he lay with her; for she was purified from her uncleanness: and she returned unto her house."

King David, who should have been leading his troops into battle according to 2 Samuel 11:1, instead chose to remain in Jerusalem. I have heard many preachers, teachers, and pastors attack Bathsheba for taking a rooftop bath. We must place the blame on the person of power, the shepherd of this story King David, not the lamb, Bathsheba. Matthew Henry's Concise Commentary says something exciting concerning David, which is, "He had not, like Job, made a covenant with his eyes, or, at this time, he had forgotten it." He goes on to say that, "See how the way of sin is downhill; when men begin to do evil, they cannot soon stop."

The truth is Bathsheba was following the law as outlined in Leviticus 15. Bathsheba was required to remove uncleanness at the eventide, which took place at sunset and was the beginning of the Hebrew day. Bathsheba would be guilty if she were bathing at noonday or any time other than specified by the law, I would like to think people who say she seduced David to have some credible evidence. But "eventide" means, according to Strong's Exhaustive Concordance of the Bible is, "Through the idea of covering with a texture, to grow dusky at sundown." She was at her appointed place at her appointed time. David was not.

A second point to consider is that women had few rights in ancient times. She had no choice but to sleep with him. David was well versed in the Law of Moses, and I'm sure he knew why she was bathing at that hour. I'm pretty sure he wished he had known that the first few days after a woman's' menstrual cycle is prime time for a woman to get pregnant. (That's just food for thought.)

Back to the story. Lastly, David was well acquainted with Bathsheba's husband.

As we saw previously, Uriah was one of his closest warriors. It was not like David didn't know Bathsheba, or he had never seen

Bathsheba before (maybe not in the manner he saw from the rooftop), but it does appear that neither Bathsheba or Uriah were strangers to David.

Bathsheba was the granddaughter of one of David's chief counselors, Ahithophel, her grandfather, and her father was Eliam, who was one of David's thirty mighty men, according to 2 Samuel 11. With her father and Grandfather positions of authority, David knew them intimately, and Bathsheba more likely grew up around the palace of David.

Bathsheba name at birth was Bathshua, which means "daughter of my prosperity." Her name Bathsheba denotes, "daughter of an oath." One writer said that her name change showed her father's appreciation of her. Bathsheba first name was in honor of her father, prominent and prosperous position in David's kingdom. The changing her name to "daughter of the oath" or "daughter of the oath-bound covenant shows a change of heart as he seemingly had gratitude to God for his daughter. Some people may feel her obedience to a man who had the power to put her and her family to death for rejecting him was consensual because the Bible does not make mention of her rejecting David's advances toward her. Only God truly knows her heart in the matter.

Truth is we all make mistakes. You are not your mistake, but they do shape who you will become, depending on your beliefs.

Regardless of what was in Bathsheba's heart at the time of their conjugal visit and David indiscretions, she became pregnant, and her husband Uriah was not the baby's father. Now we bring Uriah back into the picture.

Uriah

Here is where Uriah enters the story. 2 Samuel 11:5-11 said:

"[5] And the woman conceived, and sent and told David, and said, I am with child. [6] And David sent to Joab, saying, Send me Uriah the Hittite. And Joab sent Uriah to David. [7] And when Uriah was come unto him, David demanded of him how Joab did, and how the people did, and how the war prospered.

[8] And David said to Uriah, Go down to thy house, and wash thy feet. And Uriah departed out of the king's house, and there followed him a mess of meat from the king. [9] But Uriah slept at the door of the king's house with all the servants of his lord, and went not down to his house. [10] And when they had told David, saying, Uriah went not down unto his house, David said unto Uriah, Camest thou not from thy journey? why then didst thou not go down unto thine house? [11] And Uriah said unto David, The ark, and Israel, and Judah, abide in tents; and my lord Joab, and the servants of my lord, are encamped in the open fields; shall I then go into mine house, to eat and to drink, and to lie with my wife? as thou livest, and as thy soul liveth, I will not do this thing."

David sees the consequences of his choice. Bathsheba is now pregnant. The fact that David did not question who the father was is a testament to the character of Bathsheba. She was not known for being unfaithful to her husband. There is no record in the Bible until this incident nor afterward of Bathsheba being with another man. None other than her husband until David and none after him. David knew if not corrected, Bathsheba will be found guilty of adultery and executed. David could lose the respect of his citizens and soldiers, and he would die for his sin. These fears were not without merit. First, because they had violated the Law of God. Secondly, the people spoke of stoning David once before. In 1 Samuel 30:1-6 NKJV said,

"And it came to pass when David and his men were come to Ziklag on the third day, that the Amalekites had invaded the south, and Ziklag, and smitten Ziklag, and burned it with fire; [2] And had taken the women captives, that were therein: they slew not any, either great or small, but carried them away, and went on their way. [3] So David and his men came to the city, and, behold, it was burned with fire; and their wives, and their sons, and their daughters, were taken captives. [4] Then David and the people that were with him lifted up their voice and wept, until they had no more power to weep. [5] And David's two wives were taken captives, Ahinoam the Jezreelitess, and Abigail the wife of Nabal the Carmelite. [6] And David was greatly distressed; for the people spake of stoning him, because the soul of all the people was grieved, every man for his sons and for his daughters:"

The people esteemed the Laws of God higher than the position of king. David feeling the weightiness of the situation, decides to bring Uriah home from battle to cover his sins. According to the Pulpit Commentary:

 "Uriah, as one of David's thirty-seven heroes, would hold a high rank in the army, though the statement given by Josephus, that he was Joab's armor bearer...David sends for him, on the pretext that he wanted full information of Joab's plans, and the state of the army, and the progress of the siege of Rabbah."

We know very little about Uriah. Honor and loyalty meant a lot to him. His name translated means 'God is light.' Uriah was so eager to meet with King David that he goes to the palace still soiled from travel and war without stopping at home first. After David questioned him about the status on the battlefield, the state or the army, only listening with superficial interest to the chronicles of the war, he sends Uriah home to get rest and refreshed. By refreshed, I mean getting to know his wife like Adam knew Eve after the journey.

David tried everything he could think of to get Uriah to have sex with his wife, so he would believe Bathsheba was carrying his baby. Uriah, unwittingly, foiled every attempt. As a last resort, David planned Uriah's death. The plan he devised was not an original plan. It was one he learned from his late father-in-law King Saul. Earlier I mentioned that Saul got jealous of David's fame. Saul tried to kill David, and this was one of the methods he employed.

A lesson from King Saul.

King Saul sent David off to a heated battle during at which time he expected the young leader to die. He was sure David would not be returning. David being a gifted soldier, survived and became more popular amongst the people. David applied the same tactic David against Uriah, Bathsheba's husband. He sent Uriah to the front lines of a heated battle, and he died defending his family and homeland. David alone was responsible for the death of Uriah. Second Samuel 11:14-15 says,

"And it came to pass in the morning, that David wrote a letter to Joab, and sent it by the hand of Uriah. And he wrote in the letter, saying, Set ye Uriah in the forefront of the hottest battle, and retire ye from him, that he may be smitten, and die."

David's desire to ensure Uriah's death led him to give irrational orders. Believe me, as soldiers, we are, at times, give orders that may not make sense or go against what we feel. Emotions have little to no room on the battlefield. You must, at the time, you execute, overcome the objective, and return to base.

It is normal to reflect upon your mission. As the weight of your actions settles in, guilt will forge a place in your mind. You must charge that guilt back to the God. Thank God for:

Thank Him for rendering you guiltless.

Thank Him that you desire to protect your country, family, and friend.

Thank Him for his love, grace, and peace.

Thank him that you are free from the shame of the event but proud to be a soldier.

At this point, David was the Commander and Chief of Israel. Uriah, dedicated and loyal Israeli soldier, carried his death warrant to his commanding General Joab. General Joab followed orders as any good military officer would, which left his subordinate dead. Who is at fault for Uriah's death? It wasn't Uriah; he was just following orders completely obvious to the plan and heart behind the order. Was it Joab? He did not question David's orders to send Uriah to the front lines. Leaders are not always aware of why their higher-ups make a certain decision, so we can't blame Joab. No, God did not hold Joab responsible. He, as with Uriah, was only following orders. Where you ever given orders which you felt was wrong, but you executed them anyway? God charged David for Uriah murder. Why? Murder was in his heart when he devised the plan to kill his loyal subordinate as if he had not stolen enough from Uriah. David took Uriah wife and his life. This honesty presented in this story is one of the reasons I love the Word of God. God did not hide David sin so that the world would only see that great parts about him. The Bible shows us his faults so that we may learn from them, understand God's reactions, and grow in our relationship with Him and ourselves.

David's action is a specific example of the true meaning of the sixth commandment. The word and root for murder in Hebrew is Ratsakh is R-Tz-Ch and used here to describe how David pre-meditated and planned with malice the death of Uriah to cover his sin from the people around him. He could have hidden it from his subjects, but he was unable to hide it from God. He sent Uriah on a military mission to his death to protect his power.

It is not unusual for soldiers today or former soldiers to find themselves on missions in which you are clear on the objective but unsure of the true purpose for that mission. It's always with high hopes, and great expectancy troops make a sworn allegiance to serve and protect their nation. You trust the upper echelons of power are operating in integrity. Every mission designed to support our belief that America goal to provide equal rights for all global citizens and not power for a selected few. You spent time training for missions. You trust the mission you're sent to accomplish for the greater good. Frontline warriors are not always privy to the heart, nor do they truly understand the underlying purpose behind the orders given, but God does.

You are not responsible if you later discover a mission you executed was personal for the leader's gain and not for the greater cause you expected to accomplish. Forgive yourself because that is not your burden to carry. If you were the order giver, then repent and ask God forgiveness. The apostle Paul shared that where sin abounds grace much more abound. Let the grace and love of God fill the shame and pain you are holding. You will meet with the same grace David found in the latter part of his life.

Until this point, David focused on growing and protecting his nation. He shifted his focus to the roof of Uriah's house. David was a great soldier and leader. He has killed tens of thousands of men in battle over the years, but it was for the good of the nation or the leaders he had served. The murder of Uriah was not to further the nation or protect his kingdom. David gave the death orders to cover his sin. I was a volunteer teacher in the Florida penal system and heard the same line of thinking that some felt they had to kill to cover up their sin. What was worse is the truth that David did not plan to repent for this murder.

God sent a prophet to let David know the act of murder, and the intent of his hearts are visible to Him. David knew the effects that battle and the death had on soldiers from both sides of the battlefield. He knew how it affect families. It was his father concern for his brothers that brought David to the battlefield in the first place. What pain it must have caused the remaining members of Uriah's family who was grieving for Bathsheba deceased husband and friend. Bathsheba genuinely mourned because she loved her husband, Uriah. He was a brave and courageous fallen soldier. God did not hold Bathsheba responsible for sin of adultery at nor the murder of her husband. 2 Samuel 11:27 says, "And when the mourning was past, David sent and fetched her to his house, and she became his wife, and bare him a son. But the thing that David had done displeased the LORD." God held David responsible. After Bathsheba finished mourning Uriah, David took her for his wife. 2 Samuel 12:15-20 NKJV says,

"[15] Then Nathan departed to his house. And the Lord struck the child that Uriah's wife bore to David, and it became ill. [16] David, therefore, pleaded with God for the child, and David fasted and went in and lay all night on the ground. [17] So the elders of his house arose and went to him, to raise him up from the ground. But he would not, nor did he eat food with them. [18] Then on the seventh day it came to pass that the child died. And the servants of David were afraid to tell him that the child was dead. For they said, "Indeed, while the child was alive, we spoke to him, and he would not heed our voice. How can we tell him that the child is dead? He may do some harm!" [19] When David saw that his servants were whispering, David perceived that the child was dead. Therefore, David said to his servants, "Is the child dead?" And they said, "He is dead." [20] So David arose from the ground, washed and anointed himself, and changed his clothes; and he went into the house of the Lord and worshiped. Then he went to his own house; and when he requested, they set food before him, and he ate."

David was quite philosophical about the numerous other deaths that he caused in addition to killing Uriah's to cover his sin. David reaction was out of character for him as he is normally more concerned for his men. It was a spiritual low point in David's life. God did forgive David for murder, but he still had to suffer the consequences. The child Bathsheba was carrying died. David repented, and God forgave him. It's worth repeating that the Apostle Paul said the where sin abounds grace much more abounds. We all need the grace of God.

In the life of David, we can see the difference between murder and killing. As a soldier, when David had to take a life regardless if was following orders or giving them, it was not considered a sin in the eyes of the priest and prophets of God. That has not changed, so you should not hold it against yourself today. Even if you were angry, scared, frustrated, or any other of a wide range of emotions we as soldiers' experience in the combat zone, it is still war and grace will cover you, but you must be honest with yourself and God. If, on the other hand, you devised a plan to kill someone and you are in a sober state of mind meaning able to distinguish right from wrong and still commit the murder, please confession and repent before a loving God. He will help you to deal with the guilt, shame, and consequences of your action. David wrote Psalms 51 after he had Uriah murdered. Psalms 51 says:

"Have mercy upon me, O God, According to Your lovingkindness; According to the multitude of Your tender mercies, Blot out my transgressions. ² Wash me thoroughly from my iniquity, And cleanse me from my sin. ³ For I acknowledge my transgressions And my sin is always before me. ⁴ Against You, You only, have I sinned, And done this evil in Your sight—That You may be found just when You speak, And blameless when You judge. ⁵ Behold, I was brought forth in iniquity, And in sin my mother conceived me. ⁶ Behold, You desire truth in the inward parts, And in the hidden part You will make me to know wisdom. ⁷ Purge me with hyssop, and I shall be clean; Wash me, and I shall be whiter than snow. ⁸ Make me hear joy and gladness, That the bones You have broken may rejoice·⁹ Hide Your face from my sins, And blot out all my iniquities. ¹⁰ Create in me a clean heart, O God, And renew a steadfast spirit within me. ¹¹ Do not cast me away from Your presence, And do not take Your Holy Spirit from me. ¹² Restore to me the joy of Your salvation, And uphold me by Your generous Spirit. ¹³ Then I will teach transgressors Your ways, And sinners shall be converted to You. ¹⁴ Deliver me from the guilt of bloodshed, O God, The God of my salvation, And my tongue shall sing aloud of Your righteousness. ¹⁵ O Lord, open my lips, And my mouth shall show forth Your praise. ¹⁶ For You do not desire sacrifice, or else I would give it; You do not delight in burnt offering. ¹⁷ The sacrifices of God are a broken spirit, A broken and a contrite heart—These, O God, You will not despise. [18] Do good in Your good pleasure to Zion; Build the walls of Jerusalem. [19] Then You shall be pleased with the sacrifices of righteousness, With burnt offering and whole burnt offering; Then they shall offer bulls on Your altar."

God is a covenant-keeping God. He said if we confess our sins, he is faithful and just to forgive us. As you yield to Christ and let him into your life, he will live through you, bringing health and healing. I would like to conclude this chapter with a poem I wrote about eight years ago.

It is a key in my recovery from PTSD. The poem is titled

Tell Me How the Sonrise

To the cross, you went for me

On that day, I did not see

From His pores, he bled for me

Drops of love to set me free

Not that I deserved to be

It was the father's heart

From the cross, he cried for his father

Satan laughed and said why bother

In hell, you'll lift your eyes no further

And there you'll stay with me

Until this day I can't explain

How a few days in death brought eternal gains

Yet I still hear him calling my name saying

Arise, Arise, Arise

So, in the morning when I open my eyes

And heaven ask me how does the Son rise

I say by his sacrifice from sin I am free

I've died to myself, so He can rise in me.

CHAPTER 10: POST-TRAUMATIC GROWTH

In the article titled, General Mattis Next Mission Destroying the PTSD Myth, writer William Treseder shares a few questions posed by General Mattis. "What if instead, we could look forward to rapid growth as we heal from our wounds stronger than ever before? What if we could rebuild ourselves, and all we needed was the loving support of those around us and a little bit of time?" He goes on to share a rarely used term, Post-Traumatic Growth. General Mattis said that soldiers could return from combat and experience Post-Traumatic Growth, meaning soldiers, "Come back from war stronger and more sure of who you are." Treseder goes on to say in his article that as many soldiers and former soldiers, including myself can attest that "Growth after trauma is how we train to become physically fit and mentally capable of working together as a combat-effective team." Treseder says it like this,

"Break down, repair, break down, repair, break down, repair. It's a natural cycle, which offers a well-trod path to progressive improvement."

I'm not trying to imply there is a simple fix to the challenges of PTSD. Here a tool to work through it. Try to reframe your experience seeing the survivor you have become, not as a negative but a positive.

Dave Sanderson shared in his TEDx Talk a simple but powerful formula (he said he learned it from Tony Robbins), which is: Meaning=Emotion=Life. In other words, the meaning you attach to something produces the emotions of your life. I learned this shortly after returning from Panama.

Death in war is inevitable. War is the closes thing to hell on earth. I have experienced it firsthand. Sadly, the military never ask me if I felt it affected by my wartime experiences in any way. My near-death experiences during active fighting and the families I escorted to the military Exchange, nearly dying with multiple gunshot wounds during the Panamanian conflict was life-changing. I did not realize to what extent the war-affected me until I watch a soldier from my unit have a flashback, which is a sign of PTSD.

After returning to Fort Ord California from my deployment, a few guys from my company met up together in the barracks. We were drinking, listening to music, and trying to return to a healthy life. During our time in Panama, two army scouts from my unit were positioned forward in an observer position. While they were holding their location, they heard movement in the bushes ahead of them. The Radio back to the Command center to inquiring if we had any friendly soldiers in their area. Finding we had no soldiers in their field, they assumed the noise came from enemy combatants. The two scouts tossed fragmentation grenades into the bushes.

They later discovered what they thought were combatants were kids hiding from all the gunfire.

We knew nothing of the event until that night in California away from the battlefield. We were drinking, and one of the scouts start crying uncontrollably. When we asked what's wrong, he started screaming, "they were kids, they were only kids!" Realizing he a having a mental breakdown, one of the soldiers grabbed their car keys, I picked up the soldier and ran down three flights of stairs and rushed him to the Base hospital. We knew he was having a flashback. Once we arrived at the hospital, I carried him into the ER. A male military nurse assessed him, realizing the situation, gave him a sedative. But it was the intern's comments that hit me in an emotional place I did not know was smoldering within me. After my friend was unconscious from the sedative, the nurse said, "I wish I could have gone instead of staying in the rear." He repeated this several times. As he spoke, I thought back to what I had seen and experience lives lost. My friend on an ER stretcher and I looked indirectly in his eyes and said, "If you get me a .45 pistol, I can give you a firsthand experience!" as I felt tears of anger rising within me. I had no qualms about killing him on the spot. He bought the lie that war is glamorous and something to be desired. I irrationally thought that bullets piercing his flesh would change his mind quickly. Bring a soldier back to the civilian environment physically do not mean they can soon return mentally. It was not my best moment. I responded to him in a very livid aggressive tone causing me to realize I'd better learn to get a handle on this new sore spot within or I'm next on a stretcher. The other scout a months later bought a handgun, stood on the barracks steps and started shooting at random soldiers (his friends) he too was drunk like the first scout. We believe he was trying to commit suicide by cop. Fortunately, no one was injured; he was safely taken into custody and received treatment.

Meaning=Emotion=Life

I realized that John Wayne or Rambo war movies have no real place is a soldier's life. That is where I got my view of what it meant to be at war. The glamor of war in movies make people long for what they don't understand. The truth be told from first-hand experience, there is nothing glamorous about war. The horrors of war far out weight any calming satisfaction of killing bad people, as seen in Hollywood movies and video games. Rambo made being a soldier exciting. After the war, I was emotionally angry, which flow out of me when listening to the nurse at the hospital. I had to reframe my war experience, pulling out leadership lessons, and focus during adversity instead of anger. I'm still a work in progress. Twenty-five, plus years later, I continue to strive to help other soldiers as well. We must work on our perspective. One researcher said concerning the factors that contribute to PTSD,

"I think it is a very important thing to understand that when your friends are wounded or dead, it's a real loss. It's a loss of your friend that you trusted and you loved in a very intense way."

The study included soldiers from the Vietnam War to the current wars in Iraq and Afghanistan. Soldiers have been fighting the effects of war since the biblical days. Sadly, as we earlier discussed that nearly 8000 veterans per year kill themselves struggling between who they were and who they became after their experiences. We looked at some of the soldiers in the Bible, followed by some of the effects war has them soldiers themselves.

Elijah was one such soldier and prophet of God who experienced PTSD. Elijah began the journey of rebounding from PTSD. Here we're going to look at how God helped him to move forward healthily. What did God do to help Elijah deal with PTSD?

1 Kings 19:4-18,

"But he went a day's journey into the wilderness, and came and sat down under a broom tree. And he prayed that he might die, and said, "It is enough! Now, Lord, take my life, for I am no better than my fathers!" [5] Then as he lay and slept under a broom tree, suddenly an angel touched him, and said to him, "Arise and eat." [6] Then he looked, and there by his head was a cake baked on coals, and a jar of water. So he ate and drank, and lay down again. [7] And the angel of the Lord came back the second time, and touched him, and said, "Arise and eat, because the journey is too great for you." [8] So he arose, and ate and drank; and he went in the strength of that food forty days and forty nights as far as Horeb, the mountain of God. [9] And there he went into a cave, and spent the night in that place; and behold, the word of the Lord came to him, and He said to him, "What are you doing here, Elijah?" [10] So he said, "I have been very zealous for the Lord God of hosts; for the children of Israel have forsaken Your covenant, torn down Your altars, and killed Your prophets with the sword. I alone am left, and they seek to take my life." [11] Then He said, "Go out, and stand on the mountain before the Lord." And behold, the Lord passed by, and a great and strong wind tore into the mountains and broke the rocks in pieces before the Lord, but the Lord was not in the wind;

and after the wind an earthquake, but the Lord was not in the earthquake; [12] and after the earthquake a fire, but the Lord was not in the fire; and after the fire a still small voice. [13] So it was, when Elijah heard it, that he wrapped his face in his mantle and went out and stood in the entrance of the cave. Suddenly a voice came to him, and said, "What are you doing here, Elijah?" [14] And he said, "I have been very zealous for the Lord God of hosts; because the children of Israel have forsaken Your covenant, torn down Your altars, and killed Your prophets with the sword. I alone am left; and they seek to take my life." [15] Then the Lord said to him: "Go, return on your way to the Wilderness of Damascus; and when you arrive, anoint Hazael as king over Syria. [16] Also you shall anoint Jehu the son of Nimshi as king over Israel. And Elisha the son of Shaphat of Abel Meholah you shall anoint as prophet in your place. [17] It shall be that whoever escapes the sword of Hazael, Jehu will kill; and whoever escapes the sword of Jehu, Elisha will kill. [18] Yet I have reserved seven thousand in Israel, all whose knees have not bowed to Baal, and every mouth that has not kissed him."

How did God help Elijah's deal with PTSD?

God does not practice medicine like doctors. He perfects it. God first prescribed some rest and healthy eating. The body needs nourishment and rest before the mind can focus on any other issues. In 1905 the treatment for 'shell shock' was a few days of comfort, then soldiers return to duty. After a few days of relaxation, God began a dialog with Elijah. He assessed where he was mentally and emotionally. God listened in intently (not passing judgment), just listening.

Next, God made sure Elijah was listening before he began to counsel him. Elijah was fearful of his enemy Jezebel. He was paranoid that death would meet him, and nobody is left to defend him. Elijah felt alone. He felt death was on his heels, and there was no way of escape made for him. He had forgotten about all that God had done on his behalf. God did not attack his faith or lack of faith. From a civilian perspective, Elijah was having very irrational thoughts, but the first thing God did after listening to Elijah was to prioritize his issues. Seeing his fear of death as his most pressing issue, God addressed it first. God did not immediately relieve him of duty. He had other prophets whom he could have sent to minister to Elijah, but God loved him enough to do it Himself. He could have sent one of the hundred prophets from Obadiah's cave. God was not angry nor upset with Elijah for running. More importantly, God did not despise or rebuke him for wanting to die or running scared. God lovingly addressed him in a still small voice. That is one of the many things I love about God. As big as God knows about the billions of people on the earth today and yet He knows everything about me and wants to spend time with me. He loves you, and He is willing to do the same for you.

When Elijah was ready to return to work, God sent him on another mission with no killing required. Concerning his fear of being murdered by Jezebel, God put people in place to protect Elijah. First, he anointed Hazael as king over Syria. Next, Elijah anointed Jehu as the next king over Israel. Finally, he anointed Elisha to replace him as the voice of God to his people.

The plan was simple. Kill Jezebel & company. It is a perfect example of M-O-T and H-R-G. H-R-G meaning to take a life in a non-criminal context or a righteous kill in self-defense or when defending the innocent, in this case, Elijah.

Elijah is protected. Whoever escapes the sword of Hazael, Jehu will kill; and whoever escapes the sword of Jehu, Elisha will kill. As the Bible says that God is an ever-present help in times of trouble.

Concerning Elijah's loneliness, God let him know that He still had 7000 people in reserve in Israel who had not bowed to Baal.

Lastly, God gave him a protégés for him to train but also for protection. How do we know he was for protection? Elisha is a big strapping farm boy plowing with twelve yokes of oxen. The second key to know other than his size and later when he stayed and burned his oxen, was the statement from God that if Jezebel or her people escape the first two kings, Elisha will kill them before they reached Elijah. In addition to protecting Elijah, Elisha became a friend to him. Gene Getz said in his book, Men of Character: Elijah: Remaining steadfast through Uncertainty, "While God was helping Elijah regain perspective...God had chosen him to join Elijah in dealing with Israel's sin (see 1 Kings 19:17). But God had another purpose in choosing Elisha to serve with Elijah. Not only would he assist him in the ministry, but he would become a faithful "attendant" and, most of all, a true friend [v. 21]."

He goes on to say about the meeting between Elijah and Elisha, "Part of God's healing process for Elijah's depression involved this very thing. He provided Elijah with a dedicated and faithful man who could help him carry his burden—a man Elijah could trust implicitly. How long these two men traveled and ministered together is unknown. However, something significant happened immediately to Elijah. His depression subsided when Elisha joined the team."

All the things God did for Elijah as he struggled with PTSD, we now see as the foundation for PTSD recovery today by modern medicine. The experts say that recovering from PTSD is an ongoing process. But there are healthy steps you can take to help you improve and stay well.

Discover which ones help you and work them into your life.

One of the first keys they recommend is to connect with friends and family. The Mental Health America website says, "Studies show that having meaningful social and family connections in your life can have a positive impact on your health and healing." A person who has PTSD needs to relax in whatever healthy manner works for them as individuals, be it listening to music, reading a book, or taking a walk. Make sure you avoid using social drugs, alcohol, or smoking to relax. Listening to the Bible in MP3 or audible format is an excellent choice.

Exercise is a vital part of getting healthy as it helps to relieves tense muscles, improves a person mood, sleep, and boosts your energy and strength level. Make sure you try to exercise consistently. By doing so, you can ease symptoms of anxiety and depression.

Make sure you get plenty of sleep. The experts say that getting seven to nine hours of sleep per night help to cope with our problems better. Proper sleep also lowers your risk for illness and helps you to recover from your day to day stresses.

I would like to close this book with a quote from the late veteran Chris Kyle's book, American Sniper: The Autobiography of the Most Lethal Sniper in U.S. Military History. It is, for the most part, my belief that I embraced long before I ever heard of him, but he embraces what I hope you have drawn from this book:

"I am a strong Christian. Not a perfect one—not close. But I strongly believe in God, Jesus, and the Bible. When I die, God is going to hold me accountable for everything I've done on earth.... I believe the fact that I've accepted Jesus as my savior will be my salvation. But in that backroom or whatever it is when God confronts me with my sins, I do not believe any of the kills I had during the war will be among them. Everyone I shot was evil. I had good cause on every shot. They all deserved to die."

From one veteran to all who served, read this book, or serving in the military, thank you for serving. Remember, God loves you more than you will ever know.

Jesus said in John 15:13-14, "Greater love has no one than this, than to lay down one's life for his friends. [14] You are My friends if you do whatever I command you. 1 John 3:16 says, "[16] By this we know love, because He laid down His life for us. And we also ought to lay down our lives for the brethren."

God understands your challenges. His desire for you to seek him out like Elijah, acknowledge the reality of your trauma. It is okay admitting to yourself, to God, that you are hurting and in need of healing. David said in Psalm 62:8 to Trust in him at all times, you people; pour out your hearts to him, for God is our refuge" (Psalm 62:8). He is the key to your healing and know I'm praying for you. Amen!

NOTES

Scriptures quotation marked AMP are from the Holy Bible, Amplified Bible Copyright © 1954, 1958, 1962, 1964, 1965, 1987 by The Lockman Foundation
The King James Version of the Bible was originally published in 1611

https://www.biblegateway.com/passage/?search=Genesis %204&version=NKJV;TLB 3 January 2016

Tuesdays with Morrie: an old man, a young man, and life's greatest lesson

Mitch Albom - Doubleday - 1997

American sniper: the autobiography of the most lethal sniper in U.S. military history

Chris Kyle - Scott McEwen - Jim DeFelice - W. Morrow - 2012

Elijah: remaining steadfast through uncertainty

Gene Getz - Broadman & Holman – 1995

Men of Character: David: Seeking God Faithfulness

Gene Getz - Broadman & Holman – 1995

American sniper

Warner home video – 2015

Get rich or die tryin', Jim Sheridan - Jim Sheridan - Jimmy Iovine - Paul Rosenberg - Chris Lighty - Terence Winter - Paramount Pictures Corporation - 2005

THE MAN IN THE ARENA Excerpt from the speech "Citizenship In A Republic" delivered at the Sorbonne, in Paris, France on 23 April, 1910. http://www.theodore-roosevelt.com/trsorbonne-speech.html 6/19/2016

https://www.military1.com/army/article/461498-general-mattis-next-mission-destroying-the-ptsd-victim-myth/ 03/12/2018

I want to thank you for purchasing this book. I apologize if you found any error. If you find any mistakes, please e-mail the issue and chapter location so I can revise it before the next printing. My E-Mail address is: DRCLRILEYSR@GMAIL.COM

Please write or email Dr. Carlton L. Riley for Book Reading, Speaking and teaching engagements at:

Dr. Carlton Lewis Riley Sr.
GOD, ELIJAH AND PTSD
PO BOX 40621
JACKSONVILLE, FLORIDA 32203-0621
or
Drclrileysr@gmail.com

www.ingramcontent.com/pod-product-compliance
Lightning Source LLC
Chambersburg PA
CBHW070705250726
48662CB00001B/258